Praise
Marching Aro

"I am delighted to recommend this book. Reader get ready for your life to change. If you read this book carefully and do what it says, you will see powerful breakthrough happen in your life and in your marriage! You will see the ground shake and walls come down. I truly believe this! There are so many nuggets of wisdom all throughout the book, so please read and re-read; go through the chapters slowly and do all of the journaling. You will be sowing into your future and your marriage as you do so. Lynn is a personal friend and co-laborer in Christ. Everything she wrote came from a place of love, personal experience, and hard-won battles. This book represents years of marching around the walls of Jericho and now this is a roadmap for you to do the same. There is victory for you! I am so excited to hear the testimonies that will come from this book. Enjoy the ride, you'll never be the same."

— **Ann Hansen**
Pastor and author of *Foundations of Freedom*

"I read this book cover to cover and could not put it down. As someone who has been on fire for the Lord for quite some time, this book equipped me with newfound revelation and tools to deepen and strengthen my relationship with the Lord. *Marching Around Jericho* will challenge you to reach further levels in your faith. If I could go to my church and hand every believer this book, I would. Whether they are in an unequal yoked marriage or not, every Christ believer needs to go through this step-by-step journey of the Jericho March. The heartfelt stories are well articulated and crafted with godly wisdom. Lynn ultimately created a must read and how-to guide for every believer."

— **Patty Tower**
author at pattytower.com

When I think of Lynn Donovan, two phrases immediately come to my mind: "She loves like Jesus loves," and she, not only talks the talk, but she walks the walk." In her book, *Marching Around Jericho*, Praying Your Unsaved Spouse into the Kingdom, these two phrases will edge their way into the hearts of every reader as Lynn traces the steps she took as she marched around the walls (the harden heart) of her unsaved spouse. Being in a spiritually mismatched marriage myself for over 40 years, my faith was renewed for my husband's salvation from the things I learned from

Lynn's march, and the changes I needed to make in my own spiritual walk. I was met with a challenge to have a greater intimacy with my Father, as well as my husband. Lynn's mountain-moving steps resulted in a surprise ending that will surely inspire, teach and encourage anyone standing in the gap for an unsaved spouse.

— **Martha Bush**
author of *Helping Hurting Children: A Journey of Healing, Winning Them With Prayer* and at SpirituallyUnequalMarriage.com

"Lynn Donovan's personal journey is a stunning example of a life of faith, earnestly applied and developed as she sought the Lord and intentionally responded to His revelations. It's a much-needed example for every Christian, especially in the days in which we live. Many people seek the Lord, some learn to discern His voice, but how many intentionally respond in obedience? As you'll read from Lynn's experience, obedience can be painful, yet has tremendous rewards. Without obedience there is no breakthrough. Lynn's story clearly reveals it is our own personal transformation within that changes our circumstances outwardly—as we grow in our understanding of who God is and embrace who He says we are, His power, authority, and love is activated in and through us. I greatly appreciate Lynn for her willingness to share her journey and prayerfully believe the enemy will be pressed back, releasing many, as Christians follow her example. Praising God, believing greater manifestation of His transforming love will be evident through the lives of those who apply the instructions and principles in this book."

— **Pamela Christian**
author of the multi award-winning *Faith to Live By*
book series, radio and television host
PamelaChristianMinistries.com

When I read early manuscripts of "Marching" I was immediately impressed and drawn in. Lynn has included personal reflections from her journey seeking God's will and outlined them in practical, faith affirming steps. By blending in her own experiences, she's at once transparent as well as encouraging, using Scripture and prayers just as she learned to use them in her own faith walk. Her winsome guidance gives readers a clear path toward seeking His will for their loved ones. Riveting and affirming, I predict readers will be abundantly blessed as Lynn leads them in "Marching Around Jericho."

— **Beverly Nault**
Christian author and freelance editor

marching around
JERICHO

Praying Your Unsaved Spouse into the Kingdom

LYNN DONOVAN

THREE KEYS PUBLISHING
Books to Live By

Published by Three Keys Ministries
Temecula, California, U.S.A.
www.threekeysministries.com
Printed in the U.S.A.

Book cover and interior design by Designer Girl Graphics

This book is dedicated to every Christ follower who faithfully prays for the salvation of their loved ones. *Well done, good and faithful servant!*

Thank you, Father, Jesus, and Holy Spirit.
What a ride!

I cannot stop telling about the wonderful things I have seen and heard. — ACTS 19:20 NLT

Acknowledgements

Thank you, Sue Parks. Your faith is my faith.

To my children, Caitie and Brad. You have my heart. THANK YOU.

Mike Donovan, I love you. Thank you for allowing me to share our life together, publicly. Your courage, self-awareness, your strength, and faith, inspire me every day. THANK YOU!

Dineen Miller, my co-marcher-in-arms through the years. I adore you. You hold a piece of my heart belonging only to you. THANK YOU. And thank you for such a beautiful book design. WOW!

SUMite NATION: You are a people after God's own heart. I count it a privilege to have walked this journey with you. I will greet each of you one day face-to-face. And I'll tell Jesus that you learned to love. THANK YOU.

Bev Nault, you read every manuscript I sent your way and loved them all. I'm so glad you read this one. THANK YOU.

Denise Harmer, editor-in-arms. THANK YOU.

My local church leaders and my brothers and sisters in Christ. Your love and honor mean more to me than you will know this side of heaven. THANK YOU.

Bill Johnson, Eric Johnson and Bethel Church and every pastor, teacher and friend who poured truth into me throughout my life, THANK YOU.

Table of Contents

YEAR FOUR: *Marching With POWER*

YEAR FIVE: *Marching Practice*

YEAR SIX: *Fire Marchers*

YEAR SEVEN: *The War March & The Glory Realm*

CAPTIVES SET FREE: *March 14*

Introduction

The Lord is not slow in keeping his promise, as some understand slowness. Instead he is patient with you, not wanting anyone to perish, but everyone to come to repentance.
2 PETER 3:9

Welcome, Warrior!

If you are praying for the salvation of your unsaved spouse, it is my honor to provide you with a roadmap for your march toward the Promised Land.

Marching Around Jericho is a spiritual guide. As you read through the pages, powerful and transformative instruction and equipping takes place. We follow Jesus as he leads us around the walls, imparting kingdom truths with each passing, finally arriving at the gates of the walled-off city, our spouse's unbelieving heart. After the circles in prayer are complete, we arrive fully prepared to command the walls to crumble and be removed, making a way for our spouse to step from the rubble of lies and captivity, into faith and freedom!

This is a journey of hope and one of significant challenges. But the spoils of this war become your *pearl of great price*, worthy of your efforts, each prayer you whisper, and every tear shed. The prize is love.

How do I know? I've marched around my Jericho for the past seven years. I've traversed the seemingly insurmountable mountains in our marriage, the valleys of doom and gloom, spiritual exhaustion, and faced storms that nearly toppled our bonds of holy matrimony. Yet by the grace of God, I've gained spiritual strength, a powerful prayer life, faith that moves said mountains, and authority in Christ. I've participated in miracles, healings, and uncovered truth wrapped in love. I have looked into the eyes of perfect love and experienced our triune God, intimately, through the ordinary and the divine.

In spite of the enemy's assignment to kill, steal, and destroy all that I hold near and dear, I now thrive in my marriage and am living the abundant life (John 10:10).

We, the unequally yoked in marriage, are the chosen to demonstrate faith in Christ. We've been given a unique platform to reveal Christ's love to family members who otherwise may never see Jesus. Our unsaved spouse contemplates our victories as we model the Father's unending patience, grace, and mercy. How do I know? I've lived these truths out in my married life while waiting for the salvation of my husband.

Now it's your turn. It's time to put away powerless Christianity and step into the war room. God is releasing his church into a new season: The Kingdom Era. We, the church, are called to step into a greater love, higher authority, and the fulfillment of our purpose as we prepare for the salvation of our loved ones. And the unequally yoked are on the front lines of this kingdom advancement. Unbeknownst to many of us, the day we said, "*I do*," we stepped into the kingdom practice ground, our spiritually mismatched marriage.

Our faith and marriage vows have placed us in the classroom with Jesus, the best instructor on the planet. He is our Rabbi, teacher, friend, healer, and savior. We walk with the Holy Spirit who is the super-power to our faith. He whispers truths into our broken places and delivers us from the evil one. And never forget angelic armies stand ready, they play an integral part in our march around Jericho.

You are not alone. An entire host is on alert. They merely await God's sons and daughters to awaken from slumber, deception, and fear. They are awaiting for marching orders. The time has arrived for the kingdom of God to take back the ground stolen from the heirs of Christ. We must release the captives, heal the sick, and tend to the brokenhearted. This is our divine moment in his grand HIS-story to establish his kingdom on earth as it is in heaven and bring the Gospel of Jesus Christ home and then out to the nations.

Men and women of God, I promise you this: Commit to this march around Jericho with me and God will meet you in the journey. You are destined to become a kingdom warrior who wields great power and authority. You will find hope, truth, love, joy, peace, and a powerful faith, and you will leave your children a legacy of holiness because you lived for the kingdom of God. And through all this, your spouse will see Jesus within you.

You will hear the Master say, *Well done, good and faithful servant! You have been faithful with a few things; I will put you in charge of many things. Come and share your master's happiness!*

March on, Warrior!

Meet Lynn

Take delight in the Lord, and he will give you
the desires of your heart.
PSALM 37:4

Fellow Freedom Fighter, this book is for you. I have trod the same ground, shed the same tears, but now I've learned what Jesus has been trying to tell me for nearly three decades, and I want to share these exciting practical steps with you. Thank you for offering me your trust as I share my story. I hold your confidence and faith with deep affection and highest honor. Please know I am committed to journey with you into the presence of the Lord where our hope, healing, and victories are assured.

My spiritually mismatched marriage chronicle began in a dance club in Las Vegas, Nevada. Ya, that's right! That is where I met my husband. We dated long distance for more than a year then married quickly. It wasn't the best of circumstances in which to begin a marriage. At that time in my life, I'd abandoned the faith of my Sunday school years and was living fast and furious in the badlands of the Prodigal Nation. My brokenness and the devices of Satan left great wounds and deception upon my heart. As time passed, I found myself drawn into dangerous living that nearly destroyed my relationships with my family, my Christian friends, and almost took my life.

I was a mess.

It was in the middle of my mess I met and married my husband, Mike. Our first few years of marriage were fast-paced and complicated by a whirlwind of adjustments. We lived a worldly lifestyle, focused on career accomplishments, lavish vacations, and other shallow and perishing pursuits.

And yet, a remnant of faith from my childhood remained somewhere deep within my soul. Three years into our marriage, God whispered to my sad and battered heart. A yearning birthed within to return to the Lord of my Sunday school years. And just like the prodigal son of Luke 15, I ran home to the open arms of my loving and forgiving Father.

I was home!

However, I ran home dragging along my unbelieving spouse. And to say he was very unhappy about this new "man" in my life, is an understatement.

Thus, my journey as an unequally yoked wife began. I was utterly unprepared to navigate the complexities of faith and marriage, which were opposed by vastly different worldviews. Raw hope urged me forward. I searched the Word for answers and Jesus spoke his instructions for life and marriage into my spirit. Through tough lessons I stubbornly resisted, especially in the beginning, Jesus urged my surrender to accept his wisdom and he revealed the nuances of loving my husband outside of selfishness. Following a significant number of learning seasons, I grew up. Yet, as the years passed, I continued to struggle with conflict, anger, fear, frustration, and sadness within my marriage.

Even though I frequently failed, Jesus's brilliant schooling was creating lasting change in my heart. After more than two decades of wandering, Jesus set me upon a firm foundation of faith. After I understood the significance of surrender and the advantages of quick obedience, our marriage entered a season of greater peace.

It was in this season I looked for equipping resources for women in unequally yoked in marriages, but resources were scarce apart from a few books and an occasional Christian radio broadcast. After a number of years of learning to navigate with increasing success, I launched a blog, SpirituallyUnequalMarriage.com. I began sharing my marriage and faith experiences through writing, hoping and praying others might also find hope in Jesus for their marriages. Since 2006, I've served this growing online community of believers. We walk together in faith while we pray for the salvation of our spouses.

Out of this ministry, along with my co-writer, Dineen Miller, we wrote the book, *Winning Him Without Words*. This book is filled with practical and specific keys to THRIVE in a spiritually mismatched marriage. I believe it is an inspired work of the Holy Spirit and today remains a powerful tool for anyone looking to love God and their spouse and thrive in marriage. In addition, we wrote, *Not Alone, Raising Kids in a Spiritually Mismatched Home, and Winning Them With Prayer*.

Yet, with all my years of faith and all the thousands of prayers I've uttered, my husband remained a staunch agnostic. As the years lengthened, I battled confusion and doubt. I believed the Word of God, yet as we approached our twentieth wedding anniversary, my husband wasn't any closer to God than the day I dragged him kicking and screaming into my realm of Bible-thumping faith.

And then, on October 12, 2012, in the fullness of time, God showed up.

On that day I stepped upon the Jericho path and began to march around the walled heart of my husband.

Are you curious about this march as well as the result? Well then please walk with me and we'll discover heaven's battle plan and the specific strategies for freeing the captives. This book is an instruction manual for heaven's soldiers who desire to impact their spouse with the love of Jesus Christ. This is a truth guide to bring the church out of slumber, deception, and distortions that keep us locked in bondage, pain and unanswered prayer.

This journey leads to love.

This is our freedom march!

My dear friend, this march is our high and holy calling— choosing obedience, trusting our Father's wisdom, offer thanks in all circumstances, and yes, to witness the salvation of souls.

March on, Warrior! We win!

Lynn

CHAPTER ONE

Warrior March!

No one will be able to stand against you all the days of your life.
As I was with Moses, so I will be with you; I will never leave you
nor forsake you. Be strong and courageous, because you will lead
these people to inherit the land I swore to their ancestors to give
them.
JOSHUA 1:5-6

Freedom Marcher, there is a Godly plan for your marriage and for the salvation of your spouse.

I call it the Warrior March. As believers married to an unsaved spouse, we converge onto this path arriving from vastly different avenues. We are united in our common beliefs as well as similar struggles. The love of God unifies when we are resolute in our petitions for the redemption of our spouse. Desperate for God's love and help, we arrive at a point of no return, which propels our steps forward onto this march around Jericho. We are steadfast in our loyalty and determined to witness Jesus touch a heart closed off to God.

My friend, this pathway of faith is larger than a mere unbelieving spouse's salvation. It's our entry into the heavenly realms where we encounter Christ's glory and experience his miracles! Yet, the road is booby-trapped with lies, infested with the dogs of hell, and crawling with every manner of demonic entrapment. Our journey will not be an easy one. Satan rises to defeat us at every turn. But never fear, God will not abandon his children, not for one second. Indeed, he provides enforcers to help defend and protect us along the way.

Readiness prayer for the journey ahead:

Father, in the name of Jesus, I step boldly onto this Warrior March. I am determined to lean fully upon your truth and the leading of Jesus as I seek the salvation of my spouse. Today, raise a ring of holy fire of protection around me. Forbid the enemy from interfering in my marriage. Protect me from distortion, fear, weariness, and all assignments intended to deter my final march of victory.

Father, bless my family, home, and marriage. Release from heaven your great favor over the seasons ahead as I learn to march in step with you. Also, I ask for acceleration in my faith-life and childlike belief. Reveal your truths and release me and my family from the lies and deceptions of the demonic.

Bless me with courage, favor, provision, laughter, and teach me how to participate in the miraculous and the divine. Assign mighty battle angels to my life and family. Lord, bring about the full salvation of my family and create a legacy of powerful faith that continues for a thousand generations. In Jesus's name, AMEN.

TRUTH MARCH

Then you will know the truth, and the truth will set you free.
JOHN 8:32

Our journey around Jericho is also a truth march. We will battle for territory through awareness of biblical truth versus deceptions of the devil.

The majority of my march consisted of displacing deceptive mindsets and lies. I'm convinced seventy-five percent of spiritual warfare is stepping into awareness and out of deception. The remaining twenty-five percent, well, that is faith and prayer.

Together, we'll battle through false belief systems, religious mindsets, doubt, apathy, fear, and displace false identity. Expect the cheers of heaven each time we step out of a lie and become fully aware of God's truth, his whole truth.

Now as we prepare to march, my fellow comrades, allow me to equip you with a brand-new warrior tool belt. It's called the Belt of TRUTH (Ephesians 6:14). We'll add various supernatural tools to the belt throughout our march. Depend upon it. Strengthen and build your marriage and your faith with the tools you gain.

Truth number one: God loves you. He adores you. Did you know, you are his favorite? God is proud of you. He longs to spend every moment of every day with you. He is desperate for you to experience his goodness in daily life while in continual communication and awareness of his presence.

Truth number two: You are forgiven. The circumstances which brought about your marriage to an unbeliever are irrelevant to God. If you have asked the Lord's forgiveness, he forgave you. IT IS FINISHED! (John 19:30) You are fully forgiven and living under the covering of Christ Jesus. You are entitled to God's love and favor upon your life and specifically your mismatched marriage. God doesn't hold grudges and he will never condemn or make you feel guilty because of your past mistakes, upon seeking his forgiveness. So, if you are struggling in this area of your faith or if you have received condemnation about your marriage to an unbeliever from others, or even from a pastor, this is your freedom day. Hallelujah!

Forgive them. Forgive yourself. Release all words of disapproval to the Lord. Pray and ask the Lord to remove all shame and guilt because condemnation is a ruse of the deceiver. Your inheritance as a child of God is a thriving faith-life and a thriving marriage.

Truth number three: Our inheritance is now. God hasn't reserved our inheritance for the day we step into heaven. Freedom from fear is now. Kingdom living is now. God is releasing gifts, talents, abilities, presents, awards, and favor, along with adventures and the fulfillment of dreams, to those who hunger and thirst for more of his kingdom. The Jericho March is significantly larger than the salvation of one person. This march is our calling to search out and learn to walk in everything God desires for our life. He is incredibly anxious for us to uncover his kingdom benefits and to become the powerful children of God he knows we are. NOW!

Truth number four: God has decreed a divine purpose and destiny for your life and marriage. Each and every one of your kingdom missions, assignments, purposes, and your current season of life, were recorded in your book before time began (Psalm 139:16). They are God-given dreams, hopes, possibilities, and even mandates awaiting fulfillment. You are not disqualified because of your marital status, your gender, your age, or your socio-economic limitations, etc.

Hear me clearly: God doesn't call the qualified. He qualifies the called. We are the called. You and I are designated to be the love and voice of Jesus to a man or woman with whom we share life. We are created for a high and holy purpose. We are more than a conqueror (Romans 8:37). We have the power of life in our tongues and this truth terrifies the demonic realm.

GIFTS AND SURPRISES ARE GIVEN TO THOSE WHO MARCH

You may feel as though this march is likely to be an arduous, uphill journey in scorching heat and a 24/7 siege. Ahem, sometimes it is.

But, hear me out!

Many gifts of the Holy Spirit arrive along the way. Supernatural rest awaits when we feel weary. Relief is available when we yoke our heart and our marriage to Jesus.

I clearly recall the day God asked me these questions.

Lynn, are you willing? Are you willing to follow me, no matter the cost? Are you willing to pour yourself out as a drink offering, like my son, Jesus? (Philippians 2:17) My child, are you willing to pray for one man your entire life, even if you reach 85 years of age? Are you willing to forgo preaching to large crowds, forgo missions to the jungles of Africa, or serve the homeless because I asked you to stand for one soul? Do you love me enough to stand for your marriage and pray for the salvation of one person without any public acknowledgement or any human accolades? Are you willing to pray and serve because I love this one person with all of my heart? Isn't this what you sing about in your churches? Is this not the cry of your heart? Do you not say to me, "Lord, I will go anywhere, I will do anything for you"?

So, I ask you, my child, are you willing to love and give yourself to me for this one life?

Tears flowed as I fell to my knees and whispered a trembling, "Yes, Lord. Finally, I am willing."

It was then I began to experience realms of the divine and so will you!

Let's pray and allow the Lord to affirm your decision and bless your life and marriage.

Father, I am willing to go where you need me. I am determined to serve in this vital mission for my spouse's heart. I lean into you fully. Surround me with your love, wisdom, and strength. Walk with me around my Jericho. Teach me to love unconditionally. Empower me to discern your voice. Equip me with your battle strategies that I might war effectively for my spouse, home, family, and myself.

Bless our family. Bless our home. Seal our marriage covenant in the heavenly realms. Defeat every attempt of the enemy to delay my march. And bless me with wonder, health, vision, and strength as I seek encounters with your love, grace, and mercy. In the powerful name of Jesus, AMEN.

My Jericho Journal

DATE: _____

Today, write out your hopes, dreams, and share your struggles. Surrender it all to Jesus and commit to him your trust in your home and marriage.

_____

_____

_____

_____

_____

_____

_____

_____

_____

_____

_____

_____

_____

_____

_____

_____

_____

_____

_____

CHAPTER TWO

Wilderness, Walls, and Lessons

God is faithful, by whom you were called into the fellowship of his Son, Jesus Christ our Lord.
1 CORINTHIANS 1:9

As I write, I'm nearing the end of my seven-year march that began on October 12, 2012. In the past several months God has positioned into place a rapid succession of events in response to the many years of prayer and petition. His promises are unfolding in double time. His faithfulness is at hand.

I have waited nearly three decades to behold the hand of God as he touches the faith-life of my husband. If I could, I would point you toward a shortcut across the wilderness. There isn't one. Our lifelong journey toward heaven is centered on acquiring the skills needed to take the land God has promised for his modern-day children. However, we will discover beauty in the wilderness. God is in it. He leads by a pillar in the day and fire at night through the Holy Spirit. We need only learn to perceive God's presence in the details, listen to his voice, and invite him to be our guide and protector.

SEVEN TIMES AROUND

Now the gates of Jericho were tightly shut because the people were afraid of the Israelites. No one was allowed to go out or in.

*But the Lord said to Joshua, "I have given you Jericho, its king, and all its strong warriors. You and your fighting men should march around the town once a day for six days. Seven priests will walk ahead of the Ark, each carrying a ram's horn. On the seventh day you are to **march around the town seven times**, with the priests blowing the horns.*
JOSHUA 6:1-4 (NLT)

Each year I marched around my husband, a powerful truth emerged which profoundly changed my faith-life. Surprisingly, the majority of my march rarely involved my unbelieving spouse. In fact, I found myself alone, an eager student, participating in a divine classroom with my tutor, Jesus. With every rotation around the walls, I gained a powerful kingdom lesson crucial to the final stand in the battle for my husband's eternity. My husband was blissfully unaware of his small part in this great march. Well, almost unaware. I'll share more about that later.

Year upon year the Lord gradually transformed me. But through the slow progression, significant and noticeable changes also occurred within my husband and our marriage. Every circumference built upon the prior. The annual lessons brought me step-by-step to the day when the Lord spoke, and the walls began to crumble before my eyes.

- Year one: Intimacy

- Year two: Identity

- Year four: Power

- Year five: Practice, practice, practice

- Year six: Character, maturity, and the Courts of Heaven

- Year seven: The Glory Year and Crumbling Walls

Each section of this book expands upon these principles, allowing us to first practice, then add them to our spiritual tool belt, and finally to master. The overall purpose of our march around our unsaved spouse is designed to reveal our Kingdom identity and purpose. Knowing our identity in Christ is key to our victorious finale. Understanding my God-given identity prepared me for the battle of a lifetime, the salvation of one man's soul.

Your march will likely be different in a number of respects when compared to mine. You may march a longer road or merely a number of months depending on your individual faith journey and where your spouse is in his or her response to Jesus

In the early years, I was convinced our marriage trouble squarely rested upon my husband. Our conflicts over lifestyle choices, parenting, and entertainment, just to name a few, were "his fault" because he wasn't a Christian. I was convinced he was overly stubborn about anything faith related. I would entertain thoughts such as, *If you would only turn to Jesus, my life would be a thousand percent better.*

But that's not the way of the Father. God is far more concerned about my faith and character development than my comfort. His highest and best for my life was to learn to live as his child. God wanted my eyes focused only upon him and willingly submit my spouse's salvation to his timing and purpose.

WARRIORS CREED

Marching Warrior, our time is now. Press into the lessons ahead. They will be the foundation we build upon to increase our faith, impact our children, change atmospheres, and reveal Jesus to our unbelieving spouse. When you need a word of encouragement, go back and revisit the chapters, repeat the prayers, and read the scriptures. Take advantage of the additional resources available at marchingaroundjericho.com.

Pray without ceasing!

Behold, today it's my humble honor to commission you: Kingdom Warrior! I bless you with a fresh anointing of the Holy Spirit and affix all the rights, privileges, and responsibilities originating with this great honor. In Jesus's name, amen.

Let's march!

My Jericho Journal

DATE: _____

Today, write a prayer from your heart. Share with God your fears, expectations, and desires. Your journal entries are your stone markers, a memorial of the triumphs of God in your life and marriage. One day you will return to this book and behold the miracles you experienced during your march around Jericho.

*So Joshua called together the twelve men he had appointed from the Israelites, one from each tribe, and said to them, "Go over before the ark of the Lord your God into the middle of the Jordan. Each of you is to take up a stone on his shoulder, according to the number of the tribes of the Israelites, to serve as a sign among you. In the future, when your children ask you, 'What do these stones mean?' tell them that the flow of the Jordan was cut off before the ark of the covenant of the Lord. When it crossed the Jordan, the waters of the Jordan were cut off. **These stones are to be a memorial to the people of Israel forever.**"*
JOSHUA 4:4-7

_____

_____

_____

_____

_____

_____

_____

_____

YEAR ONE
Marching into Intimacy

CHAPTER THREE

Intimacy with the Father

*God is faithful, by whom you were called into the fellowship
of his Son, Jesus Christ our Lord.*
1 CORINTHIANS 1:9

I was seated in my home church auditorium waiting for the start of Sunday service. My Bible rested, open, upon my lap. I was stuck on a story which turned over and over in my mind, Mark 5:25-31. The woman with an issue of blood.

If you remember this woman's story, she defied the social constraints of the time. Despite the potential consequences of her heretical action, as she was "unclean," and a woman, she reached out toward Jesus grasping for hope. And in a sheer moment of desperation, yearning freedom from her years of suffering, pressed through the throngs of people to touch the hem of Jesus's robe.

She reached for possibility.

Possibility has a name: Jesus.

Raw faith established her miracle of healing.

As I read this passage for the third time, an uncomfortable emotion pushed to the forefront of my mind, demanding attention. As I thought about this woman's supernatural healing, an unwelcome feeling of exasperation provoked me. I faced a terrifying and uncomfortable truth: I could no longer reconcile God's Word to my reality.

You see, I truly believed every account in the Word about miracles of healing and deliverance. And as I read about this woman's story in the book of Mark, I was convinced Jesus healed people supernaturally. However, the more I contemplated this passage, the more my mind flooded with difficult questions that lacked proper answers. Out of a frustrated longing to understand, I prayed, "Lord, I believe the Bible. I mean, I really and truly believe your Word. So, Lord, where are the miracles?"

Leading up to this day with my Bible on my lap, I earnestly and faithfully attended church and wholeheartedly believed in Jesus Christ. I served in many capacities in the church, led women's Bible studies, for several years I was on staff at my local church in women's ministry. Faithfully, I rose early every morning to read my Bible. I was a woman of the Word. I prayed.

And without fail, at least once a week I pled with the Lord, "Please save my husband."

Crickets.

I was met with aching silence.

Sometimes my prayer tactics varied. I would politely "provide" God with multiple reasons as to why he should save my husband, "And save him right now, would you please." But year after long year my husband grew less interested in God and the faith-life I was building without him.

I'll admit, it's confusing to attend church for years, study the Word and believe what it says, and yet never witness any movement by your spouse toward faith. Confusion is a diversion from the pit of hell, which often leads those of us who are unequally yoked into seasons of doubt.

I wonder if you are like me. Have you prayed and fasted, pleading with the Lord, "Please do something to save this man. I can't go on like this."

Yeah? Well, you aren't alone!

I didn't know at the time, but my petition on this specific day as I pondered this miracle recorded in the book of Mark was heard in heaven. It would take a number of months to reconcile what God initiated that day and perhaps realize all the prayers I'd spoken over the years reached a tipping point. Because things began to change.

From that day forward God determined to respond to my question, *Where are the miracles?* Within a few months, and after a number of "God-incidences", the Lord sent me across several western states of America on a quest to find my answers and reconcile my experience to the truth in the Word.

I "randomly" (God-incident) visited my mother's church in Grand Junction, Colorado. It wasn't until months later I reconciled my chance visit as an actual divine appointment orchestrated by God. A guest speaker, June, stepped up to the mic that morning and shared stories of real-life, verifiable, healing miracles she witnessed with her own eyes. I'm talking about people on crutches, throwing them down and walking after receiving prayer. Others rejoiced as their hearing was restored, and still others were healed of emotional trauma by the love of our Savior. I listened with intensity, tears brimming. My heart screamed, *It's true. It's true. The supernatural of the Bible is true. God is answering me!*

In all my years of church attendance, I had only heard of a handful of biblical-type healings and they occurred somewhere off in a jungle overseas. But now, here was this woman sharing true accounts of miracles taking place in America and not far from where I lived. After the service I rushed to the front, determined to speak with June. Unknowingly, following my conversation with her, my Jericho quest commenced. My heart filled with a compelling need to personally witness the miracles for myself. I began the quest for experiential knowledge of the supernatural God of the Bible that I love. My faith demanded I encounter Jehovah-Rapha, the God who heals. My desire flared into passion. My course became clear. I determined to discover the realities promised to every believer in the Word.

THE COUNTDOWN

Then shall ye go and pray unto me, and I will hearken unto you. Then shall ye seek me and find me, when ye shall search for me with all your heart.
JEREMIAH 29:11 (KJV)

After leaving Colorado and returning to my home in California, I found myself in a season of growing hunger to experience God. I began to think about our Father, Jesus, the Holy

Spirit and what the Bible teaches is possible for believers. I read the Word with new insight and meditated upon passages that revealed the Lord's character. I wanted to know God, really know him. I wanted to experience what I'd been reading about in the Word for years. I wanted to witness the miracles June described.

During this "hungry season" I was also reading biographies about the great men and women of faith in our Christian heritage such as Charles Finney, Martin Luther, Kathryn Kuhlman, and Maria Woodworth-Etter. I was reading every book about Jesus and healing that I could get my hands on. I lingered in prayer, asking the Lord to reveal himself to me like he did with the great Kingdom warriors of the past.

Little did I realize on October 12, 2012 my Jericho March initiated. It was on this day God answered my heart's cry with a paradigm-shifting experience. I encountered his presence and love in a physical manifestation.

Three days prior, my writing partner, Dineen Miller, and I visited the same church June had spoken about when in Colorado. Bethel Church is in Redding, California. Together, Dineen and I attended a conference, *Open Heavens*. We hoped to understand just what an open heaven looks like.

I remember the succession of events that I experienced as if they happened yesterday. On the final day of he conference, with my arms raised in worship, singing with abandon and completely lost in the love of God, something I'd never experienced or even understood occurred.

A sensation, as close as I'm able to describe, similar to a mild electric pulse began moving in waves from the top of my head to the bottom of my feet. The pulses would hit the floor and bounce back up to the top of my head, then back down. With each wave I felt this electric power course through my body. Accompanying each wave, I could "feel" God's perfect love course up and down, up and down. The waves of love and power grew with intensity upon each pass. I began to tremble under the increasing sensation. The room disappeared from my conscious mind. I was oblivious to anything other than the overwhelming love of Father God. The shaking of my arms and legs increased to the point I could no longer stand. I crumpled to the floor under the flood of supernatural affection. I knew unequivocally this was God. He was revealing his presence and love to me through a beautiful physical encounter.

Kneeling on the floor I felt wrapped in love, light, and Holy Spirit power. Up until this point, my life's experience lacked a grid for what I was feeling. Yet, I knew God was responding to my heart's cry to know him. Within this experience the Lord brought to my mind the story I'd recently read about the revivalist, Charles Finney's shaking and trembling encounter with God. This became an anchor for my experience.

Nearly thirty minutes passed as I trembled under this flow of love and electric sensation. The worship set drew to a close and God gently subsided his loving encounter. But from that moment on, I would never be the same. I knew that I knew that I knew, in my knower, God was real. He was powerful. He was love and his desire is that I experience him intimately.

CALL ME DADDY

And without faith it is impossible to please God, because anyone who comes to him must believe that he exists and that he rewards those who earnestly seek him.
HEBREWS 11:6

Out of this holy encounter I was immediately launched into my first lesson, intimacy. As I walked along the exterior wall surrounding my husband's heart, I began to change.

After returning home, I spent hours and hours in prayer and study unpacking everything God revealed at the conference as well as what he was unfolding in his Word. In this process the Lord challenged a significant number of religious mindsets and faith traditions I held but didn't line up with the God of the Bible. The largest stumbling block rose before me one Monday morning as I began to pray. This was my moment of no return.

The Lord summoned me to surrender every doubt about him and choose to believe he is truly good, all the time, and in every way, a good Father, and he desired to live in intimacy with me. I'd struggled for years to place complete trust in the Lord because my past was littered with experiences which told me the opposite: No one is trustworthy. Thus, I remained unconvinced God could be fully trusted. However, on a chilly Monday morning in December of 2012, the Lord whispered these words to my heart, "Call me Daddy."

Gulp!

It was almost too much.

NO WAY. I wouldn't DARE call God—Daddy. This request glared in the face of a lifetime of religiosity, fear, and distrust.

Why would God ask me to call him Daddy?

This wasn't going to be easy because, well, to put it bluntly, I have father issues. Please hear me. I hold my earthly father in the deepest love and respect. He was a good provider for our family and a great businessman but often absent from my childhood. I know he believed in God, but I don't recall much more than Sunday church attendance in his life. I grew up in a safe but often performance-driven atmosphere. I also grew up in a home where little girls weren't a priority. Okay, I'm just being authentic. The message I received as a child was that I must earn love, especially from a father. From Daddy.

It's common for most people to relate to Father God based on your formative years and interactions with your earthly father. I recognize that most parents are broken people and often children misperceive their parents' intentions. Sometimes parents are woefully lacking in skills and/or the desire to lovingly cultivate the heart of a developing child. As Kingdom Warriors, there is grace and forgiveness for broken parents.

However, my insecurity issues developed from my childhood and lack of a healthy self-esteem, which influenced the many poor decisions I made as a young woman. My issues were also a factor in my decision to marry an unbeliever.

But in this moment alone with God, he began to reveal that my father issues had unknowingly created a barrier in which I kept God at an arm's length distance.

The Lord lovingly began shining light upon the consuming fear that controlled me. He revealed how fear of rejection hindered everyone, even God, from accessing the vulnerable space in my heart. Because of my woundedness, I refused to hand over to anyone the power to disappoint or hurt me at my core.

Hang in there. Sheesh, vulnerability is personal.

The reality of this moment crystalized. If I acknowledged anyone as my daddy, I was inviting the potential of experiencing devastating pain and rejection. And I simply wasn't willing to risk it. Fully surrendering my heart represented the deepest level of intimacy. I clinched my grip to the belief that the person I would dare to name Daddy would never fail to protect me, would always provide for me, and with vigilance, guard my heart. Also, my dad would be genuinely interested to know the real me, the good, bad, and ugly. My dad would love and accept me right where I am and would be there to comfort me when I face pain. He would delight to listen to me, acknowledge my voice and opinions, and would also enjoy just hanging out together, doing nothing. In my mind, a trustworthy dad is curious about what makes me giggle, desires to participate in my passions and share my dreams.

On that frosty morning in December, I realized that I needed a Father like that.

Sitting with my prayer journal, I pondered and attempted to pray. I was motionless while the internal conflict raged. There I sat, pen in hand. Yet, I couldn't write, "Good morning, Daddy," in my prayer journal. I battled myself to trust God with the tender and sacred place in my heart. I battled a lifetime of religion that said God was distant, mean, and absent.

Yet, here is Lord, the Almighty, who is asking me to cross over to him into a love relationship that feels unfamiliar and a bit scary. But this crossing might prove as the best thing that could ever happen to me.

As I prayed over a period of several days, the Holy Spirit was in continuous motion, cleansing my heart and spirit. God's truths were wiping out the lies about his character, which blocked my full trust. The conflict within played out in a moment-by-moment facing of my fears and the healing of my soul. God was asking me to surrender to him, a request of heroic proportions. A surrender of distrust, control, fear, and self-reliance. A tearing away of the falsehoods of my past and religion that failed to align with the truths God shared during my prayer time and through his Word.

The monumental moment arrived while I was seated in my prayer room five days later on a Friday morning. I reconciled the truths that God is truly a good Father and thus was absolutely trustworthy.

Boom!

The dam broke, and through tears, the breakthrough peeled off years of fear, insecurity, false beliefs, religious practices, and distrust.

I immediately arrived at the edge of an enormous cliff. Symbolically, of course, but I imagined myself standing on a precipice of a cavernous drop-off. And out there somewhere in the misty, gray, nothingness, my Father God waited. I couldn't see him, but his voice called to me, "Come on, baby girl. Jump. I'll catch you. I've got you. You can trust me."

Gulp!

It was a surreal moment. I waited. I considered. I feared. And then in a second of hopeful possibility, I committed. Truthfully, I wasn't completely confident God would catch me. That's what made the leap that much more transformative. But, in that quiet moment in my prayer room, I wrote the words, "Here I come, Daddy!"

I leapt!

He caught.

I jumped in and the intimacy with my Father opened the doors of heaven to greater experiences, revelation, and love.

My dear fellow marcher, our relationship with God is the critical underpinning for our walk around Jericho. Pursuing God is worthy of every sacrifice and must become the lifelong mission of every Jericho Warrior.

He is the Pearl of Great Price.

Again, the kingdom of heaven is like a merchant looking for fine pearls. When he found one of great value, he went away and sold everything he had and bought it.
MATTHEW 13: 45-46

Hunger

Blessed are those who hunger and thirst for righteousness,
for they will be filled.
MATTHEW 5:6

As an author, speaker, and pastor, I attend numerous ministry events, prayer sessions, and church meetings. I have the opportunity to meet and talk with a good number of Christians. A really cool thing happens when I look into a believer's eyes and recognize those who possess a deep longing to know God. The hunger within them stirs my spirit. I sense their excitement and unquenchable thirst to know the Lord with greater intimacy, experience, and love. I'm drawn to the hungry in Christ.

Desire is currency of the kingdom. It drives us forward and places a demand on the promises of the Word. The Lord is moved by our powerful prayers motivated by our hunger and desire to know him.

Jesus said, "Ask and it will be given to you; seek and you will find;
knock and the door will be opened to you."
MATTHEW 7:7

Sojourners, the hungry seek God with all of their heart, mind, soul, and strength. And like King David, a man after God's own heart, the hungry forge ahead into intimacy. Worship once a week becomes a paltry offering. Country club faith-life no longer satisfies. Prayerlessness is not an option. Hungry people are willing to pay the cost to experience the deeper things of God.

What is the cost?

Those who thirst for more lay down their self-centered life and align with the plans and intentions of God. An eager man or woman commits to the path less taken to purge their lives of habitual sin and ungodly decisions. They learn to live a life of instant forgiveness and pursue holiness in earnest. It's not perfection, but it's the effort that is important in the Lord's eyes.

This is the pathway of the righteous and divine. It's an upfront cost arrangement. It's not an easy path at times, and much of the reward is a murky glimpse in the distant future, yet deep in our hearts, we must be sold out to the truth that the reward of intimacy, adventure, and the abundant life is worth the forfeiture of what once enticed. We must be convinced this future is obtainable because we catch glimpses of his presence that abides in others who have forged the path before us and we want what they have.

Don't become disillusioned if the hungry life appears promised only to a chosen few. It isn't. And because the Lord is aware of your commitment, he frequently provides samplings of the rewards that await around each turn in the path. These small tastings are well worth the journey to holiness in and of themselves. However, the Promised Land will surpass your wildest hopes and dreams. It is God's intention that we experience this kind of wholehearted living on earth, right now. So, ask!

Remember Matthew 7:7. *Ask and it will be given to you; seek and you will find; knock and the door will be opened to you.* — I love this passage because of the resulting promise. We will find. But did you catch the ending of this verse?

The door will be opened to you.

Mic drop!

Let's pound the doors of heaven down with our hunger. Let's step into intimacy with our Father. I have more to share about God's goodness in later chapters. If you struggle to view God as a good Father, perhaps there exists a number of lies and misconceptions that are creating a wall between the two of you. Read on. It's time to tear down the wall.

FATHER ASSIGNMENT

For most of us, as children, we adopt a distorted view of God and his goodness through our negative or traumatic experiences with our earthly parents. Growing up in a home with extreme neglect or harsh punishment, shame, false responsibility, performance, etc., establishes an erroneous view of love and safety. We are unaware these falsehoods exist within our heart, and yet, these distortions, when triggered, will exert a significant impact upon our relationships with God and others.

Also, if you or a family member have ever dabbled in occult or demonic practices, you may be blocked from stepping into the reality that God is a good Father. If these situations are even remotely possible, simply repent and ask forgiveness for yourself and those in your family. Ask to receive forgiveness in the name of Jesus and by his blood. Then receive his forgiveness and cleansing of your family bloodline.

Additionally, beliefs that oppose God's love or good character are blockages to authentic intimacy. Renouncing and then replacing them with truth is a powerful way to realign your view of yourself as a loved child of God. So please walk around this wall and speak these truths OUT LOUD in earnest prayer. It's time all the walls of deception bow to the name of Jesus Christ!

Pray aloud:

> *Father, in the name of Jesus, today is my freedom day. I'm choosing as an act of my free will to partner with the truth about who you are and who I am. I declare you are my good Father. Today I renounce the lie that, Father, you are distant and not interested in my life, marriage, or heart. And I declare the truth that you are passionately involved in every aspect and moment of my life.*
>
> *Father, I also renounce the lies that I have perceived you as insensitive, demanding, passive, cold, and uncaring and that you are too busy to be involved in my life and marriage. The truth about you is my declaration; you are filled with compassion, always kind, accepting, and have joy and love, warm affection for me, and you are always eager to be with me.*
>
> *My good Daddy/Father, I renounce the deceptions of the devil that you are angry, stern, mean, cruel, rejecting, and bent on impossible expectations. The reality and my truths are you are my Father and you look at me with eyes of love, patience, grace, and mercy. You offer me truth that is available every day and have a good and perfect will for my life and marriage. You also allow me the freedom to fail and will pick me up and dust me off and set me back upon the path toward my future.*
>
> *Father, it is my truth that you are tenderhearted and never controlling or manipulative. You never think a condemning thought toward me, and you are eager to speak*

to me and I am able to hear your voice. You are proud of me in every way and will never leave me nor forsake me.

These are the truths of who you are as my good and loving Father. They are written in your word and are now written across my heart for all eternity. Thank you. In the name of Jesus, AMEN!

My Jericho Journal

DATE:

It's your turn to ask the Lord to reveal himself as your good Father. Pray to our Father who is trustworthy, true, and always on our side. Ask him to reveal himself. Jump. He will catch you.

CHAPTER FOUR
Battles and Blessings of Intimacy

Whoever dwells in the shelter of the Most High will rest in the shadow of the Almighty.
PSALM 91:1

Fellow Freedom Fighter, we have faithfully walked the first circle around the mighty walls of Jericho. Understanding the lessons of each walk-around builds our awareness to a point where we are empowered to effectively battle in the spiritual realm for our faith, our spouse, our family, and our world. These foundational truths are the underpinning for our future crusade.

Warring against the enemy of God for our spouse's soul is furious and relentless. Therefore, it's imperative to add tools to our belt with each passing. Today we are placing the tool of intimacy with God into our belt and installing intimacy as a covering over our heart.

Developing intimacy with God grants divine perspective. We battle from a place of victory. The battle has already been won. Jesus assures us of this in the book of John.

These things I have spoken to you, so that in Me you may have peace. In the world you have tribulation but take courage; I have overcome the world.
JOHN 16:33

The following powerful scriptures are truth armaments

we wear as we press on toward the crumbling walls:

But seek first his kingdom and his righteousness, and all these things will be given to you as well.
MATTHEW 6:33

And hope does not put us to shame, because God's love has been poured out into our hearts through the Holy Spirit, who has been given to us.
ROMANS 5:5

Personalize this passage and place your name into it.

PSALM 91
Whoever dwells in the shelter of the Most High
will rest in the shadow of the Almighty.
I will say of the Lord, "He is my refuge and my fortress,
my God, in whom I trust."
Surely he will save you from the fowler's snare
and from the deadly pestilence.
He will cover you with his feathers, and under his wings you will
find refuge; his faithfulness will be your shield and rampart.
You will not fear the terror of night, nor the arrow that flies by
day, nor the pestilence that stalks in the darkness,
nor the plague that destroys at midday.
A thousand may fall at your side, ten thousand at your right
hand, but it will not come near you.
You will only observe with your eyes
and see the punishment of the wicked.
If you say, "The Lord is my refuge," and you make
the Most High your dwelling, no harm will overtake you,
no disaster will come near your tent.
For he will command his angels concerning you to guard you in
all your ways; they will lift you up in their hands,
so that you will not strike your foot against a stone.
You will tread on the lion and the cobra; you will trample the
great lion and the serpent. "Because he loves me," says the Lord, "I
will rescue him; I will protect him, for he acknowledges my name.
He will call on me, and I will answer him; I will be with him in
trouble, I will deliver him and honor him.

With long life I will satisfy him and show him my salvation."

God will be our shield and protector against the arrows of the demonic realm; lies, slander, doubt, and accusation. Standing in the truth that we are loved by a good Father who is intimately involved in our life is the center of our battle platform.

GIFTS AND SURPRISES

Pinnacle moments in my intimacy journey arrived through the astonishing, the humorous and as well as kooky expressions of God's voice. For example, God speaks to me specifically in the natural world as well as directly to my heart.

On a somewhat regular basis, God sends me Mylar balloons. The balloons show up randomly, never arriving via a delivery van. I am a prayer-walker. I walk-n-pray nearly every morning in the vineyards near my home. I spend an hour with God talking and listening, worshiping, singing, and frequently in warfare. While walking in the morning God delights my heart. He'll strategically place a Mylar balloon caught on a fence or simply floating just off the ground along the path for me. The balloons simply show up in surprising and unexpected places.

Consistently balloons arrive before or after significant events in my life as a whisper of affirmation or when I'm desperate for a word from God's heart. These shiny gifts randomly contain messages printed across the front or are a specific shape or color that reflect meaning and are communicative to my current season or prayer requests.

I've received balloons with messages such as, "Princess," "Baptized" (that one was for my husband), and "Angels." "*I love you,*" is upon the face of many. I receive balloons that are promises, blessings, and a good number of them are celebrations and reminders that I am a child of God and that he adores me.

I'll guarantee that God is whispering, or perhaps he's shouting for your attention through the natural world. With intentionality, tune into his voice, listen, and receive his love. He speaks through butterflies, favor in the workplace, grace and forgiveness given and received, doves on a fence or feathers falling in unexpected places. Don't limit God or put him in a box. When you believe God is amazing, he will be amazing!

And finally, the greatest of all blessings in this journey is discerning his still, small voice that speaks directly with our spirit imparting good and kind instruction. When God speaks to me, he is specific and direct. He communicates frequently by asking questions to challenge deceptive mindsets or religiosity. He is always teaching and leading me into greater love, understanding, and revelation. Learning to hear the Father's voice is a tremendous help when I pray for others, discerning specifics for their lives.

Our Father is desperate for our healing, wholeness, and he longs for his children to experience his love and goodness. The world and Satan will disappoint you and leave you broken. Turn wholeheartedly into the love of our good Father. Abundance and freedom await regardless of what your spouse believes. Merely allow him to show you his grand goodness.

How and Now

How do we walk this lesson out and step into greater intimacy with God? The following are practical steps to growing in intimacy with our Father God.

- Pray every day, asking God to open your heart to discern his voice.

- Read the Word. God speaks through his Word. The Bible is alive with multiple levels of understanding and revelation. It's a joy and an adventure to read his Word.

- Attend church weekly even if you must go alone. Fellowship with others through Bible studies. Be active in accountability relationships.

- Read books authored by Christians who teach how to discern the voice of God. For a full list, visit marchingaroundjericho.com.

- Attend one to four faith-building conferences a year. This break from your daily routine recalibrates your faith walk, redirecting your focus back onto your relationship with the

Lord. Be selective when spending your time and money. Attend conferences that will lead you closer to an encounter with his love, healing, Jesus, and gifts of the Holy Spirit. And if you can't find a conference you can afford, the next step is enough.

- Carve out time to spend with God in nature. God loves to speak to his children through nature. Walk every day if possible and pray or at least spend some time outdoors.

- Mostly, ASK! Keep on asking, and you will receive. Keep on seeking, and you will find. Keep on knocking, and the door will be opened to you. It's God's promise.

YEAR TWO
Marching into Identity

Chapter Five

Identity in Christ

Yet to all who did receive him, to those who believed in his name,
he gave the right to become children of God—children born not of
natural descent, nor of human decision
or a husband's will, but born of God.
JOHN 1:12-13

Warrior, my earnest hope for you, as we mark our first complete circle around Jericho, is that you live fully pursuing intimacy with Yahweh. I also pray the Lord hastens your journey to arrive at the finish in a faster pace than my own. Great is the plunder when the walls tumble, but even better are the treasures and trophies hidden in the dust along the trail. Don't miss the miraculous that IS this circular journey. Our travel with other sojourners and freedom fighters, partnering with the angelic, and the revealing of the divine, establishes the crowns we will one day throw at our Savior's feet.

It's glory!

The next encirclement of our Jericho March is identity. Little did I realize that a lifetime of church attendance left me woefully unaware of my Godly purpose and identity. And I know I'm not alone.

It's time to claim our rightful place in the kingdom!

Understanding who we are and whose we are is the next imperative component in our quest toward the battle for our spouse's soul. I believe that searching out and developing our identity as a child of God is a lifelong, continuous endeavor.

Over the years the Lord has graced me with new understanding and greater authority after learning from Jesus in the heavenly classrooms. Maturity in Christ opens doors in the kingdom. We are trusted with his secrets, granted entrance to greater faith realms, and we join him to further his purposes for planet earth.

Jesus THE Great Rabbi

Decades ago, when I was newly married and struggling to navigate a marriage to an unbeliever, resources for the unequally yoked were nearly nonexistent. After praying out of desperation, Jesus became my teacher. He slowly began leading me into truths upon truths, birthing a season of peace within my mismatched marriage.

You can believe me when I say Rabbi Jesus has every answer to every problem.

For most believers, relating to Jesus is easy and our love for him grows as we study the Gospels. We connect to Christ as a kind and gentle man and as the holy Son of God. We understand and respect Jesus as a servant leader and a man of grace, our Shepherd, and suffering Savior. Our salvation experience and the redemption of our sins through the sacrifice of Christ was a gift of love we earnestly accept.

Intimacy with our heavenly Father is paramount, but I cannot overstate the obvious—we must also pursue an intimate relationship with Jesus, the son.

Our kingdom identity is born out of love for Jesus who points us toward our heavenly Father, drawing us into intimacy through the Holy Spirit. As Kingdom Marchers, it's vital we remain hungry and intentionally pursue intimacy with all three beings of the Godhead.

Jesus was known to his disciples and the religious leaders of the time as Rabbi, which translated from Hebrew, means teacher. He was brilliant in the manner in which he taught his followers in ancient times as well as his followers today. Jesus is extraordinarily concerned with our understanding of who we are as a child of our heavenly Father.

So, my dear friend, welcome to the classrooms of the

Great Rabbi. Jesus intends to equip us with the entirety of our kingdom identity. My Jericho March included numerous moments of revelation and the discovery of who I am. And this revelation profoundly impacted both my life as well as my husband's.

The Warfare for Our Soul

Before we contend for the soul of our spouse, we must fight for our own.

I'm convinced every hungry believer progresses through seasons into spiritual maturity. Growing seasons and lessons are foundational to acquiring the powerful gifts of God. Each season produces profound wisdom and fruit. I believe growing into "Sonship" flows like this:

Slave – Servant – Friend – Sonship!

As kingdom kids, we are transitioning into or out of one of these areas of identity. Where do you see yourself in this process?

Upon our salvation, most believers view themselves as a slave in the service of the king. And this isn't a bad thing. This is a great place to start learning kingdom values. The scriptures are filled with passages that teach us about each season and contain the lessons we need to progress in our maturity and development.

> *"The first one came and said, 'Sir,*
> *your mina has earned ten more.'*
> *"'Well done, my good servant!' his master replied.*
> *'Because you have been trustworthy in a very small matter,*
> *take charge of ten cities.'"*
> LUKE 19:16-17

In this passage the word servant, when translated from the Greek, means bondservant. When defined, a bondservant is a person bound in service without wages, a slave or serf.

In the service of God, the slavery identity provides lessons of stewardship, grace, and responsibility. We learn how to oversee the small gifts of God within our possession. This process is a day-by-day surrendering of self. God assesses our heart motives in areas of his kingdom priorities and duties. The Luke 19 parable models stewardship and offers us an invitation to partner with God and use his resources wisely. Each season is equipping us with the truths we need for powerful living and for claiming ground previously seized by the enemy.

But there is also an insidious plan underway. The devil is determined to trip us up, block our progress, and render us into permanent, demonic slavery. Seasons of growing maturity become the proving grounds of our character: choosing truth over lies, biblical life over worldly deception, living out the lessons from the pages of his Word. Each of these seasons will demand a reckoning. We must choose truth and break all agreements with the liar.

I think the best way to illustrate the lies and the truths of our faith journey is by contrast and comparison. The demonic realm has contrived evil plans to lure us into twisted thinking, thereby leaving us stuck and repeating the same lessons. Let's consider how the devil hijacks the Godly slave identity.

SLAVE IDENTITY

God's Purpose	Satan's Purpose
humility	selfishness
responsibility	pride
kindness	arrogance
cooperation	indulgence
service	lack
removal of sins	poverty
hope	blame
self-control	insignificance
healing	bondage
joy	pain
recovery	trauma
confidence	hopelessness

Satan's poverty mindset is a corrupted belief paradigm centered around a false humility and lack—lack of possessions, lack of favor, lack of opportunity, etc. The devil creates patterns where you live in the tension of constant need.

- Finances are consistently insufficient.
- You're a slave to your job.
- It's a paycheck-to-paycheck reality.
- You cheat a little on the tax returns, or you might slip something in your bag that belongs to the office to "make up" for what you're not being paid.
- There is nothing left over, and you are always a dollar short.

Sound familiar?

I was once in the place myself. I became free from a poverty mindset through study, great teaching, significant prayer, and the renewing of my mind (Romans 12:2). I also began to understand the value of the kingdom's perspective from my slavery lessons. We will discuss renewing our minds in a later chapter.

The opposite of the slavery mindset is being a slave of Jesus Christ. When we embrace biblical truth as a child of God, we step into the reality that our Father is rich. And our desires fade over possessions and positions that we once pursued fervently. We discover that God is absolutely trustworthy, providing for our every need, to the point that generosity is our lifestyle. In this season, we release ourselves from comparison to others, the critical spirit, and the spirit of lack. As a child, we understand our service to Jesus as we gain new freedoms—freedom from fear—judgement—scarcity—lack— shame, and more.

The lessons apprehended in the slave years lay the foundation for the Lord to build upon. We MUST possess humility that we earned while silently serving our children, our spouse, our church, etc. These are challenging years when no one acknowledges our efforts and there is little in the way of accolades, and perhaps not even a simple thank you. Jesus modeled true humility and service. We need this season to become like Christ.

Jesus knew that the Father had put all things under his power, and that he had come from God and was returning to God; so he got up from the meal, took off his outer clothing, and wrapped a towel around his waist. After that, he poured water into a basin

and began to wash his disciples' feet, drying them with the towel
that was wrapped around him.
JOHN 13: 3-5

SERVANT IDENTITY

God's Purpose	Satan's Purpose
love for God	hatred
love for people	bitterness
love and respect for creation	selfishness (serve me)
servant leadership	oppression of others
honor	control of others
respect	manipulation
responsibility	witchcraft
rewards of service	dishonor
sacrifice	disrespect
fulfillment	deceit
peace	deception
security	death
integrity	disaster
worth	destruction

Servant leadership is a brilliant example of the values and nature of the kingdom of God. Take a look at this passage from Philippians:

"Do nothing out of selfish ambition or vain conceit. Rather, in humility value others above yourselves, not looking to your own interests but each of you to the interests of the others.
In your relationships with one another, have the same mindset as Christ Jesus: Who, being in very nature God, did not consider equality with God something to be used to his own advantage; rather, he made himself nothing by taking the very nature of a servant, being made in human likeness. And being found in appearance as a man, he humbled himself by becoming obedient to death— even death on a cross! Therefore God exalted him to the highest place and gave him the name that is above every name, that at the name of Jesus every knee should bow, in heaven and on earth and under the earth, and every tongue acknowledge that

Jesus Christ is Lord, to the glory of God the Father."
PHILIPPIANS 2:3-11

The astonishing portion of this passage is what the Father did in response to the servanthood and humility of Christ. **Therefore, God exalted him to the highest place...**

Mind blow!

Servant identity is a graduation up. This season is accompanied by additional responsibilities and a strong mandate to learn to love God and people well.

FRIENDSHIP IDENTITY

God's Purpose	Satan's Purpose
trusting of others	offense
confidence	division—*especially within the*
accountability with others	*kingdom*
reliability	strife
loyalty	comparison
relentlessly honest	anger
a lifestyle of forgiveness	accusation
quick repentance	laziness
quick obedience	stunted spiritual growth
gifts of the Spirit	broken friendships
Kingdom responsibilities	destroyed families
	isolation

Jesus speaks to friendship identity:

*"My command is this: Love each other as I have loved you.
Greater love has no one than this: to lay down one's life for one's
friends. You are my friends if you do what I command.
I no longer call you servants, because a servant does not
know his master's business.
Instead, I have called you friends, for everything that I learned
from my Father I have made known to you. You did not choose
me, but I chose you and appointed you so that you might go and
bear fruit—fruit that will last—and so that whatever
you ask in my name the Father will give you.*

This is my command: Love each other."
JOHN 15:12-17

This passage is our invitation to embrace a friendship with the Son of God and with people. And the words of Jesus arrive with an astonishing promise—**"and so that whatever you ask in my name the Father will give you."**

In this season of my Jericho walk, I saw Jesus as a trusted friend. I proved my friendship through consistency. In this season of maturation, I began reading passages such as John 15, and instead of thinking of them as a moralistic story, I believed they held powerful application to my everyday life. With this insight, my prayer life shifted. I would pray something like this:

> *Father, in your Word, Jesus said that as his friend, I may ask in his name and you will give it to me. Father, I am a friend of Jesus. Lord, you know that I have matured, and you also know my heart and motives. It is foolishness to seek after fleeting trinkets of this earth. Because you trust my character, I humbly apply my faith to this passage.*
>
> *Father, I stand in full faith upon this promise of Jesus. I ask that I bear fruit. I ask in your name for the door of conversation to open that I may discuss faith with my husband. Also, Lord, I place a demand on my faith, asking you to open the door of provision for us financially through my husband's employment. I ask that you bless my husband at work. Father, I ask that Mike's boss view him as a vital team member. I ask that he is regarded by his co-workers, boss, and boss's boss, as a respected employee and that his clients request him by name. I ask, Father, that you will make my husband's name respected and that he is viewed as a man of integrity. I ask you in the name of Jesus, AMEN.*

I believe God honors prayers such as this when spoken in faith.

One of the many things I find amusing about living in an upside-down kingdom is the irony. Over the many years I've served in ministry, my unbelieving husband was the one who paid the expenses to maintain my ministry. Mike has always been my greatest cheerleader, my friend, my support in my ministry endeavors, the entrepreneurial experiments that became highly successful. And some of my, ahem, crazy and hair-brained ideas that were a flop as well. *grin*

We have been quite the team. He works at his job. I pray. God provides through him. I pray for his salvation and trust while I work in the ministry in which God has placed me. It's quite comical to look back and perceive the multiple kingdom accomplishments achieved through my unbelieving spouse. Hilarious!

SONS AND DAUGHTERS OF GOD

God's Purpose	Satan's Purpose
rule and reign	confusion
kingdom advancement	deceit
saving of souls	self-hatred
freedom and deliverance for others	hatred of others
powerful prayer life	corrupted marriage truths
commanding of the angelic	gender confusion
defeating of the demonic	loneliness
creative miracles	isolation
creative problem solving	fear
wielding of power and authority	bitterness
in Christ Jesus	suicide
peace	destruction of family
joy	destruction of the church
lavish generosity	divided allegiance
wholehearted living	self-focused love
lavish love	

Our Jericho finale will conclude as our feet touch holy ground with our Godly identity fully established.

I advanced step-by-step through each season. Some of the steps I passed through quickly; others I lingered in for longer periods. Advancement came once I determined to believe specific and challenging passages that appeared impossible or passages I believed were only available for the "super-spiritual".

However, I would study the Word, read commentaries by Bible scholars who assured that all of scripture is accessible to every believer today.

For example, with regard to supernatural healing, Jesus said:

"As you go, proclaim this message: 'The kingdom of heaven has come near.' Heal the sick, raise the dead, cleanse those who have leprosy, drive out demons. Freely you have received; freely give."
MATTHEW 10:7-8

My need to know that supernatural healing was a reality today was the pretext of my Jericho march. Along the road the Word became alive. I stepped into belief that Jesus commanded his followers to heal the sick, raise the dead, cleanse the lepers, and drive out demons. Thus, I believe as a disciple today, this verse applied to me.

I've witnessed supernatural miracles, signs, and wonders, and I expect the miraculous to be commonplace in my life. Later in the book, I share a number of these encounters. I've also participated in divine healing for myself and for others. I frequently pray for believers, and I've witnessed the love of Jesus heal people emotionally and physically. I'm aware of the spiritual gifts I carry, and through the authority and power of Jesus, I'm able to help men, women, and children walk in new freedoms and demand the tormentors to leave. The Word of God is our invitation to step into our authentic identity.

My sojourner, the enemy is seething, knowing that you are reading this book and receiving life-giving truths. But greater is he that is in us, than he that is in the world. You just tell that ole' devil to disappear into the crevice by which he came. In Jesus's name.

As children of the Most High God, it is our mandate to take dominion over our circumstances, refusing to be a victim. We are delegated to participate in divine healing, deliverance, and more. Remember, Jesus is the one who released us into our assignments when he said something utterly remarkable. Even now I grapple with the scope and reach of this verse. However, as joint heirs with Christ, it's our privilege to manifest his words into our world.

> *Very truly I tell you, whoever believes in me will do the*
> *works I have been doing, and they will do <u>even greater</u> things*
> *than these, because I am going to the Father.*
> *(underlined for emphasis)*
> JOHN 14:12

Say what???

I'm excited to ask the Lord to reveal the fullness of this passage in my marriage, family, and ministry. How about you?

Right now, ask the Lord to release revelation about these passages and ask that you begin to experience these truths in your life. Write out a prayer, in the name of Jesus, for something you know is God's will for your life but appears impossible today. God loves a good challenge!

My Jericho Journal

DATE: _____

Ask in the name of Jesus. Apply the Word and believe. Impossibility is God's specialty.

_____

_____

_____

_____

_____

_____

_____

_____

_____

_____

_____

_____

_____

_____

_____

_____

_____

_____

_____

_____

_____

CHAPTER SIX

Battles and Blessings of Kingdom Identity

Do not conform to the pattern of this world, but be transformed by the renewing of your mind. Then you will be able to test and approve what God's will is—his good, pleasing and perfect will.
ROMANS 12:2

How do we move out of a false identity and into the reality that we are children of God? We choose to believe what the Word declares about us.

We place our identity-armament upon our faith prior to stepping into the arena to fight for our spouse who is resistant to faith in Jesus Christ. We are up against more than most believers understand. And to effectively engage the weapons of our warfare, we must first apprehend and then operate out of the underpinnings of our identity. I'll share more about weaponry and warfare later.

I think there are several key components to solidifying our identity:

- Take back our thought life
- Believe the Word. The Bible unequivocally defines God's identity and our own
- Leave powerless Christianity behind and learn to partner with Holy Spirit power

- Move out of independence or self-sufficiency to complete dependence on God

- Grow from distrust of God and self to trust in both

- Worthlessness—to Worthy—to CHOSEN—to Nobility

- Move out of rejection to self-acceptance and love and acceptance by God

- Reject lies regarding our identity and embrace Sonship

An effective process to work through identity is asking reflective questions, such as: Is this thought/behavior becoming of an ambassador of the kingdom? Is this thought/behavior reflecting the heart of a powerful child of God? Journal these questions and allow Jesus to help you process the answers and lead you through the maturing process.

GIFTS AND SURPRISES

For he "has put everything under his feet." Now when it says that "everything" has been put under him, it is clear that this does not include God himself, who put everything under Christ.
1 CORINTHIANS 15:27

It's time to add another tool to our truth-belt. Kingdom identity is a game changer. Your mind will settle. Doubts flee. And through your friendship with Jesus, you become empowered to take captive all things and bring them under submission to the Lord Jesus Christ.

Identity change happens when we take our thoughts captive to Christ. So, let's learn this next lesson together.

In the middle years of my marriage, prior to understanding my heavenly identity, I would wrangle with a constant onslaught of angry thoughts. My husband would say or do something that pushed my buttons. I'm of the personality to hash things out instead of avoidance. So, when I was angry, I wanted to talk it out. My husband, well, he despises confrontation and evades verbal spats like the plague.

Our dysfunctional communication would play out in our home like this. Bam, a disagreement ensues, we exchange heated words, and then I start in on him with my frustrations and complaints—all of them. Yikes, he knows what's coming, so he's off down the hallway at a rapid pace, me following right on his heels. He disappears into his home office. I'm fuming. I head out to the garden to shovel some of my frustration.

That was until a certain summer morning, with shovel in hand, I discovered the key to my freedom.

Right there with the dirt flying, I stopped short, as beautiful awareness emerged upon my mind. Do you remember earlier I mentioned that 75% of spiritual warfare is awareness? Well, this was my moment of mindfulness and everything changed from that day forward.

Up until then, I would be digging in the garden and the same old reel of complaints, injustices, and poor-me prattling played on repeat in my mind. Over and over the words of anger boiled against this man that I loved. By the end of an hour, my garden looked great, but I was so bound up in ugly thoughts that it would take me days to unwind and subdue the pain.

However, on this day the Lord broke through. Jesus's lessons were impacting as truth arrows targeted upon my heart. I stood straight up in the middle of my garden, shovel still in hand, with realization donning upon my mind. I clearly remember whispering to myself, *Wait a minute. These thoughts circling in my brain ARE NOT nice. They are angry, mean, and cruel. And I KNOW that I am normally a happy person and generally nice. So, WOW, these thoughts aren't mine. And I absolutely KNOW they are not of God. So, they are coming from someone else.*

Whoa!

In that moment, I realized that I was listening to a demonic voice that was twisting my thoughts, filling my mind with lies, and stirring up a fierce anger against my husband. I was devastated, but also amazingly relieved by this revelation. Immediately I said OUT LOUD, "I take these thoughts captive to Christ."

Under the unction of the Holy Spirit, I raised my forefinger and pressed it against my right temple and said again, but louder, "I TAKE THESE THOUGHTS CAPTIVE TO CHRIST!" Then I flung my finger away toward heaven as if I was pulling the evil thoughts from my mind and flinging them to Jesus.

That verbal command shifted something. The evil thoughts stopped immediately.

Wow! I had discovered something here. THIS was my new secret weapon.

BECOME A LUNATIC

We demolish arguments and every pretension that sets itself up against the knowledge of God, and we take captive every thought to make it obedient to Christ.
2 CORINTHIANS 10:5

My friend, what happened next was an entire year of taking thoughts captive. Frequently the old reel of angry thoughts would creep into my conscious mind. Mostly this would occur while I was driving or in the shower. Weird, I know.

What made my newly discovered secret weapon powerful was my awareness. I was learning to recognize the "random angry thoughts" origin wasn't within me nor from God. And once aware, I merely placed my finger on my temple and spoke aloud, *I take these thoughts captive to Christ.*

I'm not kidding when I tell you that I drove around my town in southern California for more than a year and likely looked like a lunatic. Any other motorist who might be watching would glimpse this blonde lady waving her hand like crazy, spinning her finger off into space and shouting at no one in her car. Yep! Comical.

Comrades in Christ, I have a question for you. Are you plagued with destructive thoughts? Do you desire to have the mind of Christ? Well, I welcome you to become a lunatic too. I promise you that this process works. But the key is consistency, relentlessly pursuing your freedom. If you remain steadfast to change your thought patterns, Jesus will help you.

You can expect pushback from the demonic realm, but they tire quickly and give up when they realize you are serious about taking your thoughts back. It's easier for them to turn their wicked attentions toward someone who isn't battling for their mind. Besides, once you gain this powerful tool, they become fearful. Because they know what comes next.

Annihilation!

HOW AND NOW

The Practical—add this life-changing tool to your truth belt right now. The key to launch the lunatic tool is awareness. Practice until you become a Christ mastermind.

- Determine to recognize consistent thoughts that you know oppose God's truth and are conceived from a source other than your inner Christ-like character.

- Capture those thoughts immediately and say out loud, or at least to yourself, NO. These are not my thoughts.

- Then speak OUT LOUD, I take this thought captive to Christ and use your finger to spin them out of your mind and send them away to Jesus.

- Then replace those thoughts with blessings. Bless yourself with 2 Timothy 1:7, "For God did not give me a spirit of fear, but of power, love and a sound mind."

- Bless yourself with peace, aloud.

- Thank Jesus for the renewing of your mind and give him praise.

CHAPTER SEVEN

Rescue Back Our Kingdom Identity

*Jesus said, "If you hold to my teaching, you are really my disciples. Then you will know the truth, and **the truth will set you** free."*
JOHN 8:32

Gently, the sobs began. With patient love and compassion, I listened on the other end of the phone while this beautiful woman talked with Jesus and invited him to cleanse away the lies that sorrowed her heart for most of her life. The love of Jesus released her tears, healing her very soul.

Prior to this moment during our prayer session, revelation from Jesus illuminated *the* single devastating lie spoken by the demonic that held her in bondage, pain, and fear her entire life. The devil whispered throughout her childhood and into her adult years: *You are a mistake.*

The enemy of our soul is relentless in his efforts to convince us that our life is a mistake. He wants us to believe the words we sometimes whisper to ourselves: *I am a mistake.*

This woman truly believed she was a mistake. She was told she was conceived by mistake, then adopted and that was a mistake. To punctuate this lie, the enemy continually brought before her memories cloaked in shame and secrecy from her childhood that she was the mistake. Her life was a mistake. She was bound with spiritual chains to a false identity of unworthiness and rejection.

The moment Jesus spoke to her heart and affirmed her true identity, she was instantly freed from decades of lies perpetuated by the Orphan Spirit that had defined her for more than 50 years. In two short hours, Jesus revealed the truth that she is a perfect reflection of his love, favored and highly valued. She wasn't a mistake, but loved, adored, and wanted. In this redefining moment, Jesus swept away a lifetime of striving, perfectionism, fear, and judgment, then released her into truth, new life, and hope.

At long last, she was no longer insignificant, but became the truest thing about herself, a loved daughter of the King.

I am humbled and honored to pray with people and witness the freedoms that arrive when Jesus heals. Multiple Healing Prayer sessions have made me keenly aware that believers are afflicted, oppressed, in poor health, and that far too many of us settle for a mediocre life and a corrupted identity. I recognize false identity in others quickly because for many years, I was a captive of the enemy who hijacked and distorted my worth. My life was a mess of grief, regret, anger, jealousy, fear, and unrealized potential, just to name a few. I was a walking identity crisis.

Escaping a falsified identity is the next victory tool to place in our belt of truth.

RESCUED IDENTITY

Jesus replied, "Very truly I tell you, everyone who sins is a slave to sin. Now a slave has no permanent place in the family, but a son belongs to it forever. So if the Son sets you free, you will be free indeed."
JOHN 8:31-36

From conception to our return to eternity, we process every single message that life throws our way. With each event, interpersonal interaction, circumstance, and experience our human mind/heart processes, then renders decisions and conclusions, good and bad. These judgments profoundly influence our entire life and become our truth.

Truth or a lie?

Unknowingly people often process their life circumstances through cloudy lenses of deception or half-truths, concocted by the enemy of our soul. We adopt belief systems predicated on our perceptions of truth. Upon reaching adulthood, many of the beliefs we adopted don't align with the truth of the Word. At the core of our identity we live from a skewed or distorted position of who we are. We believe something different about ourselves that came through the messages we processed as truth in our childhood, but these messages contradict what the Lord says about us. Furthermore, we hold on to distorted beliefs regarding God's person and character.

This is precisely what occurred with the woman with whom I'd prayed with at the beginning of the chapter.

Praying with her further, she experienced a moment of life-altering truth. Jesus revealed to her that she was CHOSEN. Chosen by God, before time began, to be born exactly on her birthdate, perfectly woven together to have brown eyes and a kind heart, and to be loved and accepted. She was specifically designed to be a woman. She was never a mistake and all of heaven celebrated the moment she arrived in the delivery room.

Years of anguish were washed away as Jesus made known her true identity and as she forgave those who labeled her as a mistake. The enemy lost control as lies were demolished by the blood of Christ and her chains of insecurity and worthlessness were broken!

This is rescued identity.

Hallelujah!

Now let's add another instrument that releases us from the bondage of lies and bitterness.

THE PATHWAY OF FORGIVENESS

Bear with each other and forgive one another if any of you has a grievance against someone. Forgive as the Lord forgave you.
COLOSSIANS 3:13

Jericho Warriors MUST walk the road of ongoing forgiveness.

Effective warfare is waged from our awareness. Let's realize that emotional wounding upon our heart and soul frequently results in spiritual bondage. Soul wounds are birthed out of traumatic events, abuse, neglect, misunderstanding, and word curses we speak over ourselves or words spoken over us by an authority figure in our life. These are a few examples of debilitating soul injuries that linger well into adulthood. If left unhealed by the love of Jesus, they morph into a lie cloaked as truth. Lies fester in our broken heart, eventually becoming a seeping, septic, bleeding soul disease. This spiritual infection releases dysfunction into multiple areas of our physical, spiritual, and emotional being. Demons lurk within these seeping abscesses, causing havoc in our lives and relationships.

Forgiveness releases us from the bondage of bitterness and the demonic strongholds in which they inhabit. Our soul is healed when we forgive ourselves, others, and when we forgive God.

Walking in a lifestyle of quick forgiveness is crucial to bringing down the walls that surround our Jericho. I believe I've discovered an effective process to unwind the lies. Forgiving others of their transgressions enables us to release the bitterness trapped in our soul. You might be thinking to yourself, *I've already forgiven so and so.* However, this process is different. There are several components that not only release forgiveness, but also bring about healing.

Begin by engaging your voice. Pray out loud. The words spoken aloud by a daughter or son of God engage the heavenly realms and the angelic move upon your prayers.

Pray: Jesus, I choose to forgive (<u>person's name</u>).

I forgive them for (<u>list each offense, be specific. Ask Jesus to reveal the wounds</u>).

Because it made me feel (<u>speak each emotion here, aloud</u>). Take your time. Journaling this prayer is recommended.

Jesus, cover these wounds with your blood and heal by your stripes. I forgive and release (<u>person's name</u>) from these offenses.

Now, Jesus I ask you to bless (<u>name</u>). This is when you choose to view the person through the eyes of Jesus and perceive their brokenness, background, difficult upbringing, failures, and need for a Savior. Bless them (or their memory if they have passed) with…(<u>speak everything they need or that you would like to give them and bless them to know the love of our Father</u>).

Finally, pray and thank Jesus for freeing you from the bondage of bitterness, anger, hatred, confusion, etc. Get it all out. Don't withhold anything from the love of Christ. Finally, speak aloud and pray; I receive your forgiveness, Jesus, and I break all legal rights of the demonic and I command all spirits of bitterness, anger, hatred, confusion, etc., etc. to go directly to Jesus and never return.

In the powerful name of Jesus, AMEN

I use this tool often. I forgive everyone of everything. I use it the second I feel offense rising. Offense is another dastardly weapon of the enemy. If the demons can keep us offended, they hold the upper hand. In fact, recently the Lord said to me, "Lynn, the second you are in offense against anyone, you're in sin."

Yikes!

I realize that this is a simplified prayer model and the wounding in a human heart is often deep and complicated. Sometimes people are unable to gain breakthrough from oppression without help from others. I encourage every believer who has dedicated significant time praying for breakthrough and is yet to receive it, please seek assistance from someone experienced in healing and deliverance prayer. Your freedom, health, purpose, and your joy await. Don't delay another day.

Call your local healing rooms, healing prayer rooms, prayer ministries at your church, or contact me and schedule a Healing Prayer appointment through marchingaroundjericho.com. Ask Jesus to reveal the right person to pray with you. Seek your wholeness because your freedom becomes a key and a doorway first for you, and then for others to step through and experience victory.

Bear with each other and forgive one another if any of you has a grievance against someone. Forgive as the Lord forgave you.
COLOSSIANS 3:13

Repentance and forgiveness are tools of the Great Carpenter, who is continually honing a human spirit into a powerful kingdom envoy. Gaining our freedom from deception and wounding brings us into alignment with the Word of God and his divine purposes. Walking in the truth of sonship is the next full circle about the walls of Jericho.

The Key of Forgiveness is already in your belt. Well done!

Ask Jesus to reveal names and/or any unhealed offenses, pain, or trauma. Release your past to Jesus. Write a prayer on the next page dedicating yourself as a child of God who walks the path of ongoing forgiveness and love.

My Jericho Journal

DATE: _____

This portion of the journey is non-negotiable. Dealing with soul wounds and unforgiveness is essential before we take one more step. If we are unhealed and walking in bitterness, the enemy knows this and will use our wounds to hinder future battle prayers for our unsaved spouse.

Make time to work through forgiveness of parents, siblings, other family members, perpetrators, co-workers, etc. who have harmed you. Forgive yourself. Forgive God. Ask Jesus about those who may still need forgiveness; if certain names come to mind, chances are, you still have forgiveness work ahead. There is liberty in wholeness. There is victory for every believer who processes through the hard work of forgiveness.

Also, pray through the prayer of forgiveness of your spouse found at marchingaroundjericho.com

Don't rush the process. Seek others to pray with you if you are still blocked or unable to move out of unforgiveness. P.S. Share this powerful forgiveness tool with your children.

_____

_____

_____

_____

_____

_____

_____

_____

_____

CHAPTER EIGHT

The Spouse Effect

What, then, shall we say in response to these things? If God is for us, who can be against us?
ROMANS 8:31

I've written several chapters about developing intimacy and identity because everything we acquire through the chapters ahead rests upon these two pillars of faith. Before we move on to the next tool for our victory belt, I want to share how these foundational supports have an impact on our faith, home, spouse, and marriage.

As I began to develop intimacy with Father God, I noticed a shift first in me. Out of intimacy within my morning prayer time, I began to experience increasing peacefulness. I *feel* tangibly and physically, the presence of God abiding within and around me throughout the day. Prior to this season, I would pray in the morning and then start on my tasks for the day without a thought about God, his desires, hopes. I was completely unaware of his voice.

When I finally began to practice continual awareness of God's presence, I recognized his presence and his voice while cooking in the kitchen, writing in my office, driving in my car, and working in the garden. These were practice sessions. Because as I matured in his teaching, this also began to happen while in conversation with my husband. The Lord began coaching my heart toward my husband over a lunchtime sandwich, for example. Mindfulness of God's continuous presence changed my perception of living. Instead of looking continually to my husband to affirm me and my purpose, the Lord spoke gently to me with his goodness and affirmations and I was able to communicate with Mike without losing my temper or rushing to the garden to furiously dig weeds.

In response, the Lord opened my spirit to recognize the enemy's interference in my relationship with my husband. The Holy Spirit clued me in about areas of conflict that I should ignore, or those which required prayer covering and divine wisdom. This revelation from heaven birthed lasting joy and excitement. My joy became a perpetual wellspring, thereby impacting my unbelieving spouse. Abiding with God reduced conflict, irritation, selfishness in me and, surprisingly, also in my husband. My intimacy with God determined the spiritual temperature in our house. Jesus and I became the thermostat, not my husband's unbelief or worldly viewpoints.

Praying out of my relationship with the Lord released me from fear. Instead of uttering my selfish "rescue me" prayers, I began to pray blessing prayers. Wow, what an impact this kind of prayer creates in day-to-day living! God's continuous responses to my prayers increased my faith by leaps and bounds.

Every time I grew in my understanding and deepened my relationship with God, my husband was a direct recipient of the goodness surrounding me. His work and career life became satisfying because I blessed him instead of asking God to relieve me from my disappointments in him. My husband also began to feel less stressed out because I was less stressed out.

Every step into a deeper faith and understanding actually led me to love my husband with greater maturity and depth. I loved him with earnest affection because now I could view him through the eyes of my Father. And my Father adores my husband.

As I grew up into my true identity, conflicts over faith completely subsided. Mike's faith posture was irrelevant. I was having the time of my life loving God and spending every day with him. I no longer turned to my husband to fill the empty space in my heart. I remained fully assured that God loved Mike and would work everything out just because I prayed and asked.

And we know that in all things God works for the good of those who love him, who have been called according to his purpose.
ROMANS 8:28

Our conflicts over media, which were once a source of pain for me (and for him), became irrelevant. Freedom came and I felt released from all false responsibility that I needed to defend God and my faith. It mattered little to me what Mike thought about Jesus or my faith. I KNEW who I was. I KNEW God, Jesus, and the Holy Spirit. It was settled once and for all in my soul and a mere unbeliever couldn't rock the foundation on which I stood.

I became a daughter of the King. Even the demons began to tremble when I opened my eyes in the morning and said, "Good Morning, Daddy!"

This is the *Spouse Effect*. Our faith, prayers, and living in unity with the King births within us a humble boldness. We gain kingdom confidence that is communicated to others through our interactions and in many situations, without muttering a word. When we follow hard after Jesus, our influence impacts others. We open the doors of faith all around us, allowing people to catch a glimpse of glory. And they want what we possess, Jesus Christ.

*To them God has chosen to make known among the Gentiles the glorious riches of this mystery, which is **Christ in you, the hope of glory**.*
COLOSSIANS 1:27

I'm convinced that this passage is far-reaching, offering more than most believers grasp. My dear Freedom Fighter, if Christ is IN US, how then can a mere mortal stand against us?

Memorize this passage and ask Jesus for greater revelation to understand how wide, how deep, and the far-reaching effects these truths offer your faith-life and marriage.

THE FELLOWSHIP OF THE UNASHAMED

Proclaim this with me, friend:

I am part of the fellowship of the unashamed. I have Holy Spirit power.

The die has been cast. I have stepped over the line. The decision has been made. I am a disciple of his. I won't look back, let up, slow down, back away or be still.

My past is redeemed. My present makes sense. My future is secure.

I'm finished with low living, sight walking, small planning, smooth knees, colorless dreams, tamed visions, worldly talking, cheap giving, and dwarfed goals.

I no longer need preeminence, prosperity, position, promotions, applause, or popularity. I don't have to be right, first, tops, recognized, praised, regarded, or rewarded. I now live by faith, lean on his presence, walk by patience, am uplifted by prayer, and labor by power.

My pace is set. My gait is fast. My goal is heaven. My road is narrow. My way rough. My companions few. My guide is reliable, and my mission is clear.

I cannot be bought, compromised, detoured, lured away, turned back, deluded, or delayed. I will not flinch in the face of sacrifice, hesitate in the presence of the adversary, negotiate at the table of the enemy, pander at the pool of popularity, or meander in the maze of mediocrity.

I won't give up, shut up, let up, until I've stayed up, stored up, prayed up, paid up, preached up for the cause of Christ.

I am a disciple of Jesus. I must go till he comes, give till I drop, preach till all know, and work till he stops me. And when he comes for his own, He'll have no problem recognizing me. My banner will be clear."*

Amen! May it be so in our lives!

*Written by a Rwandan man, who in 1980, was forced by his tribe to either renounce Christ or face certain death. He refused to renounce Christ and was killed on the spot. The night before he was martyred, he had written "The Fellowship of the Unashamed" which was found in his room.

Year Three
Marching into
AUTHORITY

CHAPTER NINE

My Authority in Christ

"Truly I say to you, whatever you bind on earth shall have been bound in heaven; and whatever you loose on earth shall have been loosed in heaven.
MATTHEW 18:18

Well done good and faithful servant! We have traversed the first two laps around Jericho. Our relentless pursuit of intimacy with God and our kingdom identity tramped down the weeds surrounding the walls, then plowed open a visible pathway. Together, we've forged our way forward through thickets and past boulders placed around our unbeliever by our enemy. Hallelujah!

The journey becomes easier from here.

Now let's widen the pathway with a profound gift, authority in Christ Jesus.

I'll joyfully tell you that my time in the "authority of Christ" classroom rocked my world and was a favorite. I'm a perpetual student in this aspect of faith because I was created to destroy the works of the devil. Today, I serve the kingdom through deliverance and healing prayer ministries. Excitement rises within me when I pray with a son or daughter of God and watch Jesus set them free from oppression, releasing them into their kingdom identity. Praise Jesus!

Authority is our next roundabout Jericho. It's an uphill march with a steep learning curve requiring significant practice. However, once around this mountain we are distinctly prepared for the final showdown in the seventh circle.

So, battle up, Warrior. It's our birthright to destroy the works of the devil! Wahoo!

WHO IS OUR ENEMY?

But the Son of God came to destroy the works of the devil.
1 JOHN 3:8b

The primary ministry of the demonic realm is to kill, steal, and destroy (John 10:10). And my beloved friend, the devil is relentless in releasing his mission upon the children of God. In fact, if you are a Christian, you are his primary target. He's not as interested in your spouse as you might guess. Your spouse, by default, already domiciles within his camp. NO, he wants YOU. And the demonic realm relentlessly pulls at the strings of your spouse's mind in an effort to cause you to doubt God's love, truths, and provision. If successful, you'll become discouraged to the point you tire or become bored with prayer and Bible reading, then eventually turn away from Jesus, destroying all remnants of faith, declaring you a prisoner of war.

This may sound overly dramatic, but I promise, this is the sum total of the devil's ambition. However, God's aspiration is victory over the works of darkness first for yourself, then your family, and finally for others. Today I'm keenly aware of the combat strategies of God. I acquired battle acuity during the third circle, where I received the authority of Christ.

This chapter may challenge you. However, without understanding our enemy it's impossible to deliver his defeat. It's imperative we directly confront common held beliefs and deceptions about the devil and the demonic realm.

Lie number one: Demons aren't real.

Lie number two: It's impossible for a believer to experience demonic oppression or harassment.

These are two of the greatest deceptions perpetrated upon the western church today. Allow me to blow those deceptions out of the water with several truth bombs.

First, let's absorb the fact that one-third of the ministry of Jesus involved the casting out of demons. Jesus ministered deliverance to the church, not unbelievers. He ministered to the children of Israel, the keepers of God's covenants. The Gospels are replete with accounts of demons who are present and inhabiting people.

After hours and hours of prayer sessions, I'm convinced demonic oppression is the root cause of nearly all human suffering, affliction, and illness. Healing and delivering humanity from illness and oppression was incredibly important to Jesus. So much so that he endured the tortures of the cross, extending freedom from the works of the devil to all who will believe. Throughout the Gospels he confronts the demonic directly and then offers us something mind-blowingly generous—he teaches his disciples how to cast out demons and heal the sick.

My early beliefs regarding the demonic realm were born out of a church stream that believed and taught that demons weren't real nor was it possible for a Christian to be oppressed by demonic beings. But I could no longer reconcile this teaching as truth when I considered the realities I witnessed with my own eyes.

My soul wouldn't abide, knowing many of my Christian friends, after years of faith and prayer continually suffer from crippling addictions, destroyed families and broken marriages, trauma and illness. It just didn't make sense. I couldn't reconcile what I read in the Bible about the life of Jesus and his teaching. The biblical accounts weren't reality in my faith-life. But why?

It wasn't until I jumped into a significant study of the demonic realm that I began to unravel the pack of lies that held me in powerless Christianity.

Of course, the first two lies I mentioned earlier are absolutely countered by Jesus in the Gospels. Demons are very real. They are actively at work to destroy our lives today and they have been given power to affect our lives. I will explain how that happens shortly. Stay tuned.

THE BLAME GAME

And God said, "Let us make man in our image, after our likeness: and let them have dominion over the fish of the sea, and over the

fowl of the air, and over the cattle, and over all the earth, and
over every creeping thing that creepeth upon the earth."
GENESIS 1:16 (KJV)

I'm convinced that believers suffer at the hands of the demonic because we don't understand how our enemy opperates. We have lived under those first two lies for so long, and our deception is so great, that much of what is perpetrated upon the human race is blamed upon God. When in fact, it's Satan at the root of ALL suffering. We blame God because we believe that he is in control of absolutely everything.

He is. Well, God is sovereign over absolutely everything. However, at the very beginning of the human race, God assigned dominion to humankind. In Genesis chapter one Adam handed dominion of the earth to Satan. Jesus purchased it back. God hasn't changed his mind in all these years. He remains steadfast in his purpose that his sons and daughters retain their dominion over the earth. We were created to be the caretakers of this planet and release the kingdom of God here on the planet.

Thy kingdom come, Thy will be done in earth, as it is in heaven.
MATTHEW 6:10

God can and often will intervene supernaturally in our lives. But his greatest desire is to have his children, established in our kingdom identity, exercise our Christ-given authority to influence our world. That is why our mature identity is crucial to walking in our authority over the devil.

We have mistakenly believed that because God didn't show up to save us from a circumstance or handle a difficulty for us, that God failed us. When in fact, everything, and I MEAN EVERYTHING, that is wicked, hurtful, harmful, unfair, and bad is birthed out of the demonic realm. Blueprints of evil are carefully constructed for every living being and then skillfully executed to destroy and to create distrust in God. And finally, we don't exercise our authority that is inherently ours due to our lack of knowledge (Luke 10:19).

Truth bomb: Our Father in heaven is good.

He is good every day and in every way. Our belief that God is good is thrown off through our difficult experiences. Early in our childhood, through manipulation, deceit, or distortion, the demonic uses others to hurt or control us. God's divine plan for an individual and/or family becomes corrupted by evil and therefore the original design of love, kindness, and the divine family structure is nearly destroyed. The destruction of family is meticulously crafted, then designed to flow from one generation to the next. This negative cycle repeats, becoming more corrupt over hundreds of years. That is until one ordinary believer discovers the truth and gains healing in Jesus. Jesus sets them free as well as the generations that follow.

Hallelujah!

To add to the confusion, there has existed teaching in the church that the demonic realm isn't real, therefore our only conclusion is that our difficulties must be by the hand of God. It's a fallacy that has kept many in pain and far too many from healing and salvation.

Take a minute to reflect through this new lens. Are you able to discern what I just described within your life or your family generations? What about your spouse's or loved one's past and resulting present?

The vital truth to add to our belt is twofold. God is always good, and he loves us completely and desires to bless us with his goodness. Second, the truth is, we have an enemy determined to oppress and destroy everything that is near and dear. My friend, understanding our enemy is key. With our awareness, the devil loses his control and power in our lives and eventually in the lives of those we love and pray.

We must step into the truth that human suffering is conceived of the devil and never by the hand of God. We must acknowledge that as children of God, we play a vital role in defeating the enemy and it's our role and responsibility to recapture ground and release the prisoners of war.

FEAR NOT

For God hath not given us the spirit of fear; but of power, and
of love, and of a sound mind.
2 TIMOTHY 1:7

These foundational truths will challenge old mindsets
and long-held belief systems of religion. It might feel a bit scary
to own the truth about the demonic realm. However, in the Word
of God we are told 365 times, one time for every day of the year,
do not be afraid. That message is on repeat to help us realize
there is nothing to fear from evil spirits. In fact, I will attest that
the demons are terrified because you are reading this book and
discovering your authority over them. They know defeat is near
at hand.

We overcome the works of the devil when we believe
the scriptures and practice our faith, line upon line and precept
upon precept, following the examples and teaching of Jesus. Let's
take a look at how we walk this out.

Jesus told us he would give us all authority over ALL the
works of the devil.

*When Jesus had called the Twelve together, he gave them power
and authority to drive out all demons and to cure diseases,
and he sent them out to proclaim the kingdom of God
and to heal the sick.*
LUKE 9:1-2

My steps into the authority of Christ began with a simple
choice. I chose to believe, and I received authority as a disciple
of Christ over ALL the works of the enemy. Below is a prayer
crafted from several scriptures that exercise authority in Christ.
Pray aloud, daily:

*Father, in the name of Jesus, I thank you for giving
me power over ALL the power of the enemy according to
Luke 10:19.*

*I exercise that power now and I bind and break the
power of witchcraft, curses, hexes, and all demonic assignments of evil. In the name of Jesus, I bind and break the
power of every spirit from the kingdom of darkness work-*

ing against me and (names of persons or ministries, etc.-say each name). AMEN!

I break the power of every negative word spoken against me, all word curses and all accusations of evil spoken against me and (names of persons or ministries, etc.). These curses and accusations must fall to the ground powerless! In Jesus's name.

I thank you, Father, for turning every curse that would come against me or mine into a blessing. I declare the enemy must pay back, times seven, everything that has been taken or destroyed....for our good and your glory (Numbers 24:9, Romans 8:28).

I send out warring angels, according to Hebrews 1:14, to decimate all assignments the enemy has for my family, my ministries, and me this day! I bind every evil spirit with a watcher assignment, sent to gather information, cause confusion, or corrupt the works of God in my life and the lives of my family members and ministry!

Father, in the name of Jesus, I assign mighty angels to stand guard, with swords drawn, at every door and window of my home and places I minister, that nothing of the enemy will prosper. I also assign angels to travel with me and mine wherever we go.

Father, I ask that you expose any unholy activity or assignments and destroy all blueprints of evil. Grant me discernment and wisdom from heaven. Provide revelation that I might be as wise as a serpent, but harmless as a dove (Matthew 10:16), and Lord, I cover all forms of communication, written and oral, with the blood of Jesus. I bind every spirit that would carry my words with intent to harm or use them for evil... Place a cover over my mouth, lips, and tongue. In Jesus's name.

I cover myself (names of persons, ministries, etc.) with the precious blood of Jesus this day. I declare we are sanctified, set free, powerful children of God. Reveal to us this day, the kingdom assignments declared for our lives. And now I receive a fresh filling of the Holy Spirit. I ask for your wisdom and revelation to know how to bring your kingdom to earth today in my life.

    Now to you, Lord, be all honor, power, glory, love, and highest praise. In the mighty name of Jesus, AMEN and AMEN!

Let me tell you this prayer brings immediate results. Consistently after I pray this prayer, the Holy Spirit always prompts me to pray about others or issues which are on the Father's heart. It's amazing.

During my authority march, I gleaned wisdom from several books written by Christian authors that taught strategies for defeating demons through prayer. I studied and continue today to study scriptures, with a specific interest in Jesus's approach to defeating the demonic. His examples are truly impressive and we are called to emulate him by exercising our authority granted by Christ.

If you are interested in additional study in this area, and I do hope you are, find a list of suggested reading at marchingaroundjericho.com.

AUTHORITY IS BORN OF CHARACTER

For this reason also, since the day we heard of it, we have not ceased to pray for you and to ask that you may be filled with the knowledge of his will in all spiritual wisdom and understanding, so that you will walk in a manner worthy of the Lord, to please Him in all respects, bearing fruit in every good work and increasing in the knowledge of God.
COLOSSIANS 1:9-10

The depth in which you walk in authority is directly tied to the maturity of your character and faith. The greater my confidence, faith, and understanding of my identity as a child of God, the greater my authority over the demonic. I remember the day when I realized my authority in Christ was increasing. I was a regular speaker for MOPS (Mothers Of Preschoolers) in southern California. Following my teaching, I typically extend an offer to pray one-on-one at the meeting's conclusion. Usually a line of expectant faces await.

    One specific morning, a young mother asked for relief

from crippling anxiety. She was paralyzingly afraid to step into the operating room at the hospital where she nursed. When I'm praying for someone, the Lord will reveal his heart for that person to me. When I looked into her strained and fearful face, my heart welled up with love and hope for this young woman.

I began to pray and command the spirit of fear to leave. I listened intently to the Holy Spirit and I prayed as the Holy Spirit led. We prayed only a few minutes, but as I spoke, I witnessed the miraculous. The actual shape of her face changed. The demon was forced to free her, and as it fled, her stressed-out, elongated face softened and rounded before my very eyes. It's likely no one else in the room noticed, but I watched the physical shape of her face change. Also, the dilation of her eyes relaxed. I could see in the natural what Jesus was doing in the spiritual.

I said amen. She nearly knocked me down when she flung her arms around me in a desperately happy bear hug. She was teary. I was teary. It was the love of Jesus that released her that day. Many months later I received a beautiful email about the victories in her life and career because she stepped out of fear.

Warriors, we are the disciples of Christ. This kind of faith is our mandate and our privilege. It's also one of the most rewarding experiences to witness Jesus arrive and set people free. But the best experience is gaining freedom for yourself and family.

My Jericho Journal

DATE: _____

Kingdom authority is shouldered through a lifestyle of wholehearted love for God and people, submission, obedience, and quick repentance. These are the character qualities of a powerful Jericho Warrior.

This walk around the walled fortress may present you with some significant character work (prayer). Using your authority and your faith, ask Jesus to uncover any oppression that may be causing defeat in your life and that of your children and spouse.

Pray with Jesus using his name, his authority, and by his blood, break the strongholds and legal rights of the enemy. Then pray and release the opposite of what you have struggled with in your life. If you have battled fear and anxiety, bless yourself (and family members) with peace, joy, identity, truth, courage, and confidence, in the name of Jesus. If you've contended with anger, guilt, shame, unworthiness, and rejection, command these unholy spirits to leave you and take with them their works and effects, devices and weapons. Bless yourself with the opposite. In the name of Jesus.

This process is rarely a one-and-done. Often, it's our continual knocking on the door of heaven in prayer, over and again, that we obtain our wholeness. Ask Jesus for help. He died for our liberty. He always reveals areas that need healing, deliverance, and freedom.

I bless you today into a new season of truth and freedom. Your best days are ahead. March on, Warrior!

_____

_____

_____

_____

_____

CHAPTER TEN

Authority and Our Pre-believing Spouse

*Behold, I have given you authority to tread on serpents and
scorpions, and over all the power of the enemy,
and nothing will injure you.*
LUKE 10:19

Are you ready for some really great news? Standing in our authority will rapidly and powerfully change your unbelieving spouse.

I clearly remember the day the authority of Christ met the challenger that lurked behind my husband. This moment arrived somewhere in the middle of year four of my Jericho March. The dynamics in our home and family were in transition as my daughter had moved across the country to attend Purdue University for an advanced degree. At this point in our marriage, Mike and I enjoyed a generally peaceful and happy relationship. However, an occasional conflict would erupt and was presented through some kind of verbal spat.

I'm challenged in my vulnerability sharing our struggles, but the truth set me free. It's said that hindsight is 20/20, and looking back now, I clearly comprehend the dynamics at play. However, at the time of this conflict, I was only partly cognizant of the subtleties that lived within our ongoing bickering. A word spoken here. A criticism there. This was an uncomfortable reality in our married life.

However, in this season as I was learning about my authority in Christ, I recognized that several demonic oppressive behaviors were attached to me, and many were attached to my spouse. I spent hours and hours in prayer repenting, seeking deliverance, healing, and restoration over my own life. In fact, in this process I revisited a number of old conflicts from my past. I recalled a specific day when a relative, not my husband, and I engaged in ugliness. Ugh. I processed this conflict with Jesus and realized a demon of anger had a foothold in my life. This fiend of the devil somehow had a legal right to have influence over my thoughts, emotions and actions. Looking back, I could see how anger controlled many of my decisions and contributed to the strife and wickedness within my marriage as well as other relationships.

Awareness is the key. I repented, engaged my authority, and commanded that ugly spirit of rage to leave. And in the name of Jesus, anger left me. Since that day I am no longer controlled by urges of anger. Rage doesn't compel me to say things I will regret later. Warrior, if you struggle with anger—and most of us do—repent. Ask Jesus to show you the root of this oppression. Ask him to heal your soul wounds, emotions, will, mind, heart, and body. And then as a son or daughter of the king exercise your authority in Jesus's name and command the spirit of anger to go into the pit and never return. In Jesus's name and by his blood.

Fast forward, following my freedom from anger, I came to a place in my life where I couldn't abide any longer with my husband's angry outbursts, however infrequent. Typically, my husband is not an angry man. But once in a while, angry words flew about the house toward me and it felt mean and hurtful and wrong. I honestly don't think he realized the influence of this spirit in his life. However, I did. The Lord revealed to me how anger provoked him into hurting me and maintained continuous conflict within our marriage.

I would have never recognized anger in my husband if I hadn't first dealt with it in my own life.

On this specific day, I'd reached the end of living in a home with the spirit of anger. I don't remember exactly what prompted an angry retort from a simple question I asked standing in my husband's office. However, an angry and mean-spirited answer shot from his lips as I looked at him from across the desk, hiding my pained surprise. He was spitting mean words, but I was mesmerized by his face, looking at the thing I perceived hiding and laughing at me from behind his eyes.

I walked away. Calmed down. Went into my room and prayed. I commanded that ugly spirit of rage and fear to leave my husband in the name of my powerful Jesus and by his blood. I walked back into his office and said in a matter-of-fact but kind tone, "I can no longer abide with this anger that comes over you. You must get it under control, or we are in serious trouble here. I won't live with this any longer."

Now you might gasp at this demand, but in the moment, I was quite serious. It was either anger or me that had to leave, and I wasn't going anywhere! My husband is a kind and gentle man on most days. That is the man that I wanted to live with 24/7, not this angry imposter. Mike looked at me. Didn't say a word.

I left his office and since that day, anger has been banished from our life and marriage. We are living in the best season of our marriage. It is peaceful, respectful, full of honor and genuine affection and kindness. I'm convinced that my authority through 1 Corinthians 7:14 and Mike's awareness that anger was a problem was enough to break rights of the enemy.

Oh, how I wish I had known about my authority 20 years earlier!

Since then I've commanded anything and everything the Holy Spirit points out that is working to deceive or influence me, my kids, my husband, my dogs, and even my friends. And I take my authority with me on the road.

Authority in Walmart

And He summoned the twelve and began to send them out in pairs, and gave them authority over the unclean spirits.
MARK 6:7

Did you know that kingdom authority is portable? One

of my favorite places to take the authority of heaven is into Walmart.

Typical of any market, there are lines and there are people. Generally, people live life unaware of the spiritual realm or the dynamics of the kingdom of God that surround them. I find it exciting to uncover the demons loitering in public places, trying to stir up anger, division, disgust, hatred, etc. It's fairly simple recognizing their wicked manipulations when people in the checkout line begin bickering with one another.

When these tired, old ploys of the devil start, I simply whisper a prayer. "I take authority over this situation (store, checkout line, etc.) in the name of Jesus. I command these demons of strife, anger, and anything else the Holy Spirit reveals, to leave. RIGHT NOW. In Jesus's name." I wait. I watch. Sometimes I need to pray again, or even a third time. But I've observed a situation that is nearly explosive dwindle and people in conflict leave or separate.

Once I remember browsing the produce section and a woman was throwing an absolute fit because she couldn't open the thin plastic produce bag. I simply walked over to her and gave her my opened bag. I smiled and said, "Bless you." Every part of her body reacted. Her angry and contorted face first went to shock and something shifted. She smiled. She sheepishly offered a stumbling apology regarding her behavior. I turned to go and smiled and whispered, thank you, Jesus.

HE IS SO FUN.

Once, I was in the checkout line and filled up with the Holy Ghost so much so, that he was leaking out of every pore of my skin and affecting those around me. A woman whom I knew from years ago was leaving after her checkout from three lanes over. She spotted me.

We locked eyes. She rushed straight for me. Through a stumbling bear hug accompanied with tears streaming down her face she choked out, "I just need a hug." I smiled, embraced her fully. Blessed her and told her that she was loved. Her entire countenance changed. She started to giggle-cry. She thanked me, gathered her bags and children, and headed out the door. A few days later she emailed me to tell me how my simple embrace changed her day and her outlook on life.

Say what???

Is it possible for the children of God to carry that much of his love and authority? My dear friend, indeed, it's possible and we must. An entire world is at stake. Our homes and family stand in the balance.

FEAR NOT! We were made to love people in Walmart, the post office, everywhere! We were born to live extreme. Powerful ambassadors of the King, that is our destiny. This is our inheritance. This is our birthright.

It's a blast to live the believer's life. Even in Walmart.

Power Passage
of the Unequally Yoked

For the unbelieving husband has been sanctified through his wife, and the unbelieving wife has been sanctified through her believing husband. Otherwise your children would be unclean, but as it is, they are holy.
1 CORINTHIANS 7:14

In my book, *Winning Them With Prayer*, I expand in greater detail upon the spiritual importance of our faith as a believing spouse, the hierarchy of family in the kingdom of God, as well as the strength of this passage in first Corinthians.

This passage should be emblazoned upon our hearts and fixed in the forefront of our minds.

I can't tell you the number of times I've repeated this passage in prayer, stood upon it in faith, and proclaimed and then applied the truths to my husband, children, and grandchildren.

I mention this passage again because this verse is one of our primary weapons we will wield upon the battlefield in the seventh passage. This is our sword that we unsheathe, then point at the foundations of Jericho. This passage shakes loose all that can be shaken.

At that time his voice shook the earth, but now he has promised, "Once more I will shake not only the earth but also the heavens." The words "once more" indicate the removing of what can be

shaken—that is, created things—so that what
cannot be shaken may remain."
HEBREWS 12:26-27

Praise Jesus!

Soldiers-at-arms, the truth is this: God knew there would be marriages such as ours. And he did not leave us ill-equipped to navigate the specific nuances of an unequally yoked union. No, this passage is included in the New Testament just for us. It contains brilliant truths that I continue to unpack, searching out the far-reaching implications of its message and power. God intends for us to believe this passage and then behave as if we know it is true.

In my prayer time, I would pray this passage and remind the Lord that I believe in his Word with a child-like faith. I would pray something like this:

Father, in the name of Jesus, I approach your Throne of Grace this day. I'm thankful you adore me and you love my husband and family. Today, Father, I stand upon 1 Corinthians 7:14 and set a proclamation over my husband that he is sanctified and made holy because of my faith in Jesus. I also declare that this verse stands as truth over my children.

Today, Father, I apply the blood of Jesus over my husband, my children, and myself. Please protect all of us and draw us near. Lord, reveal yourself to my husband and allow him to gain the knowledge of Jesus as his Savior. Lord, I claim my husband for the kingdom of God and believe he will participate in the works and purposes recorded in his book before time began. Lord, I ask the same for my children.

In the name of Jesus, I come into agreement with you that my spouse and children are holy, chosen, highly favored, and blessed. You bless them because of my faith as I stand on your promise in 1 Corinthians 7:14. Release your love in abundance over each of us. Create unity in our home and marriage. Bless our marriage with peace, love, joy, truth, and righteousness. And Lord, let your love flow out of me that I may be a reflection of Christ in the eyes of my family. In Jesus's name, amen.

1 Corinthians 7:14. Memorize it. Believe it. Ask Jesus to unpack the depths of power and authority it offers. And above all, stand upon it for the salvation of your family.

YEAR FOUR
Marching with
POWER

CHAPTER ELEVEN

Kingdom Power

*I have given you authority to trample on snakes and scorpions
and to overcome all the power of the enemy;
nothing will harm you.*
LUKE 10:19

Standing in front of this young man, I felt a strange tingling and a warming sensation on the top of my wrist.

Six months earlier working with my garden rototiller, I accidentally ran the machine into the block wall that surrounds my backyard. The dumb thing jumped violently, throwing me off balance. I fell backward and my right wrist smacked against the wall. Searing pain screamed up and down my arm. Swelling began immediately.

Mike drove me to the emergency room. Thankfully it wasn't broken, but badly sprained. My wrist remained immobile, tender and weak for months. Six months later it was frustratingly frail. Even the weight of my handbag proved too much. Finally, I scheduled an appointment with a surgeon who looked at my MRI and said, "Yes, the torn tissues need repair."

Ugh!

Which brings me back to the young man who was standing over me, praying. With my surgery scheduled for early December, I attended the October conference, Open Heavens, which I've attended every year since my Father encounter. This particular October, I took my fragile wrist into the healing rooms, hopeful for relief.

And almost immediately, when this young man and his team members, another young man and a white-haired old woman, prayed, the sensations manifested in my wrist.

I was shocked. I looked at the young man. "I can feel it. I can feel Jesus healing me." I began to jump up and down, shouting, crying and laughing at the same time. The team started shouting, my daughter and her friend who were with me were stunned. I could feel a fascinating heat and tingling going into my wrist.

The team concluded their prayer. And Warrior friends, I left the building believing I had been touched by the Holy Spirit power and Jesus Christ. My wrist wasn't instantly healed. However, it felt better.

After a month, I noticed increasing strength and stability. With this improvement, I called my physician and postponed the surgery. I queried him about the possibility of physical therapy and agreed to surgery if the therapy didn't work. January was the earliest appointment.

I kid you not, a week prior to my January physical therapy appointment, my wrist felt normal. Holding my purse in my right hand was painless. I called the doctor and canceled all my appointments! Hallelujah!

I WAS HEALED. Supernaturally. The power of God rested upon me and I received a healing miracle.

This astonishing event occurred early in my faith journey. The third year of my walk around Jericho. In this season I was voraciously reading and studying everything I could get my hands on, learning about the power and authority of Jesus, his miracles of healing and deliverance. Why did the Lord choose to release healing power into my wrist? I'm convinced it's because I chose to believe in the possibility. And indeed, the Lord did not disappoint.

Since that time, I've witnessed the supernatural healing of others. I've prayed for others for their healing and I'm honored that I have witnessed Jesus heal them.

Year four march is our classroom in understanding and learning to cooperate with Jesus and the Holy Spirit to release supernatural power. Kingdom power is a gift that the children of

God must add to their tool belt. If we are to follow the mandate of Jesus, to heal the sick, then it's time to acquire understanding of the power that raised Christ from the grave and how it operates within a believer's life.

THE HOLY SPIRIT

*He said to them: "It is not for you to know the times or dates the Father has set by his own authority. **But you will receive power when the Holy Spirit comes on you;** and you will be my witnesses in Jerusalem, and in all Judea and Samaria, and to the ends of the earth."*
ACTS 1:7-8

The Holy Spirit's primary mission is to release kingdom power through the sons and daughters of God. This power came to humanity when Jesus ascended to heaven. And this power, the presence of the Holy Spirit, is still at work today.

Learning about the work of the Holy Spirit brought joy and wonder into my life. I felt like a giddy kid, excited about the prospect of partnering with the power of God. This was a pivotal time in my faith-life. Up until then, I believed the Pentecost baptism had died with the first century church. I can't say how this teaching became commonplace within the church. I'm truly puzzled; after all, the Bible's replete with examples of healing by the followers of Jesus.

The church has greatly misunderstood the Holy Spirit and his purpose. I think it would be helpful to lay out a few foundational truths which I discovered in my journey toward hosting the presence of the Holy Spirit.

First, I believe that upon our faith confession in Jesus we receive the gift of the Holy Spirit.

And Peter said to them, "Repent and be baptized every one of you in the name of Jesus Christ for the forgiveness of your sins, and you will receive the gift of the Holy Spirit."
ACTS 2:38

However, I hold the conviction that the baptism of the Holy Spirit is different than our water baptism of faith. The baptism of the Holy Ghost is exactly what Jesus released to his disciples when he breathed on them (John 20:22). As modern-day believers we are overshadowed and endued, provided with, power from on high. Of course, these two baptisms will often occur at the same time. For me, I became a believer at age nine, but I received the baptism of the Holy Spirit the moment the power of God fell upon me at the beginning of my Jericho march as an adult. I came away from that encounter with a knowing that something different now rested within.

Since then, I've spent several years reading and learning about the Holy Spirit and how to partner with the Spirit of God to bring heaven to earth.

I'm convinced that our identity and intimacy with the Lord is the anchor for all we do for the kingdom. Power and authority are released through our faith and our voice. I'll share more about our voice in the next chapter. Our faith releases the will of God because we hear his voice and follow his desires and prompting. The Holy Spirit, in partnership with the angelic realm, backs up our words spoken in faith. This partnership releases the miraculous and it's also how we dispatch demonic oppression.

I loved this particular year that I circled around Jericho. The Spirit is thrilling and fantastic. I was excited to wake up every morning anxious to find out how the Holy Spirit would reveal himself that day. It was fulfilling to finally witness God's response to my heart cry spoken years earlier that launched this crazy pilgrimage. In this season I received my answer. The miracles of Jesus Christ continue today and occur frequently.

Hallelujah!

Mountains of Christian teaching about the Holy Spirit, healing, deliverance, etc. abound and are authored by various writers that often contradict one another. Which further confuses the body of Christ. But, Freedom Fighter, fighting for an unsaved spouse's soul requires equipping with power from on high. It's time to put away debate and doubt. The Holy Spirit is available, and with his baptism we literally are offered the possibility to walk in the power that raised Christ from the dead.

Booyah!

The Spirit of God, who raised Jesus from the dead, lives in you.
And just as God raised Christ Jesus from the dead, he will give life
to your mortal bodies by this same Spirit living within you.
ROMANS 8:11

This verse is our truth. Tuck the possibilities into our tool belt and embrace the fullness of the Triune God. This is our inheritance and birthright.

PRAYER LANGUAGE

He said to them, "Go into all the world and preach the gospel to
all creation. Whoever believes and is baptized will be saved, but
whoever does not believe will be condemned. And these signs will
accompany those who believe: In my name they will drive out
demons; they will speak in new tongues."
MARK 16:15-17

In the weeks following my initial encounter with the Lord, I found myself at a new church. I was experiencing some brand-new elements of the kingdom since my return home that I couldn't fully comprehend or process. I found myself seeking out believers to help me make sense of these spiritual experiences. One thing immediately emerged. During worship I sensed an urging rise within me and the best that I could decipher was that the gift of tongues was rising up inside. However, I was freaked out over this aspect of faith. I didn't understand it.

Finally, one Sunday morning after service, I hesitantly asked a few ladies who were standing around to explain speaking in tongues. It's a heavenly language between you and the Lord, they assured me, and I control it. God didn't take over my body and switch something on, then off. No, the Holy Spirit is a gentleman. It was up to me to turn it on and off. I learned from these women of God that my prayer language creates opportunity for God to move powerfully. Praying in tongues edifies my spirit and is beautiful in worship. The ladies explained that our voice in tongues releases power and confounds the devil, as he could not decipher my words.

Wow!

They began to pray in tongues and said, "Lynn, you follow along and just release your mouth to emulate what we are doing." I was shocked as I heard syllables begin to tumble out of my mouth.

Since then I have developed and practice my Holy Spirit prayer language. I hear reflections that sound similar to an Arabic language at times. Often when I'm in a warring position in prayer, a Korean-sounding language will flow. Weird. But the Holy Spirit has allowed me to pray in my prayer language and I'm able to discern when a shift happens in the spiritual. And I know that God's purposes were accomplished through my obedient voice.

One time while on a walk-n-pray, I was praying intensely in tongues. And I stopped short and looked up and said, "Lord, what in the world am I saying?"

Revelation came immediately as I began to pray in English, "I praise you, Father. I honor you, Lord. I worship you, Father in heaven. I ascribe praises to your name. I love you, Father." The words spoken in my prayer language were powerful words of worship. Speaking these words of praise in English, the Lord's love and affection came upon me. I could discern and feel his love and pride in my offering through speaking in tongues.

Indeed, I know that I've warred against the demonic within my prayer language. I contend frequently in this realm for the city where I live. I contend for the ministries and the people I represent in the kingdom. I battle with my words, English and in tongues, for my family, marriage, and for the salvation of my spouse. Releasing our words in faith is just that. FAITH! I can't fully explain this aspect of our faith. However, speaking in tongues is validated in the Word.

"I will send you the Helper from the Father. The Helper is the Spirit of truth who comes from the Father. When he comes, he will tell about me."
JOHN 16:26

When Paul placed his hands on them, the Holy Spirit came on them, and they spoke in tongues and prophesied.
ACTS 19:6

Compadres-in-arms, our prayer language is another vital addition to our tool belt. If you have yet to gain speaking in tongues, ask the Lord for it. Ask for the baptism of the Holy Spirit. Seek out a believer who prays in tongues and ask them to lay hands upon you to release the baptism of the Holy Spirit and the gift of tongues.

And then practice, pray and practice. It becomes a beautiful connection to God and a powerful weapon of faith in the battle rounds ahead.

COOPERATING WITH THE HOLY SPIRIT

Those who live according to the flesh have their minds set on what the flesh desires; but those who live in accordance with the Spirit have their minds set on what the Spirit desires.
ROMANS 8:5

I'm convinced that if the children of God would merely demonstrate the power they contain within, every man, woman, and child would become sold out believers in Jesus Christ. Let me ask you this. What changes in your life might you experience if God backed up your words? Think for a moment how prayers of that magnitude might impact your spouse and family.

Jesus determined our powerful faith was worthy of his torture. He willingly endured the cross to provide us with the faith that moves mountains. And he is waiting for the children of God to simply believe and step into everything that was purchased by his precious blood.

I grieve when considering how Jesus feels when believers pray paltry, faithless prayers that lack any amount of power. I simply won't do it. SO MUCH IS AT STAKE. And we have the answer for every problem in this entire world. Jesus! We need to pray his kingdom forward.

When we cooperate with the Holy Spirit, we engage our faith with the expectation of a response by heaven. Study the Word and read books written about the Holy Spirit. Our growth of understanding, discernment, and wisdom creates confident faith. Our prayers anchored in confident faith release the power from on high. Our declarations of faith spoken over others and ourselves release healing power. Decrees stated in confident faith have the power to dislodge hordes of demons, sending them back to the pit.

The power and authority of Christ, anchored within our intimate relationship with the Trinity, centered in our identity, offers change to every aspect of our life. Our prayers release blessing, rescue others from darkness, establish hope, love, joy and peace, and perhaps in our lifetime, change the world for the cause of Christ.

Oh Jesus, let your will be done!!!

In later chapters I share examples of how my prayers of faith altered significant events in my life and that of my husband. Stay tuned!

My Jericho Journal

DATE: _____

Partnering with the Holy Spirit is a fantastic ride. The Holy Spirit is our gift sent from Jesus. His purpose is a covering of righteousness and God's whisper to our heart. The Holy Spirit is our comforter when persecution arrives. He is our power.

Kingdom authority is a portion of our inheritance as a child of God which manifests through the presence of the Holy Spirit. It's positively awe inspiring to partner with the Trinity. I won't limit or compartmentalize the Trinity. Father, Jesus, and the Holy Spirit—each person of the trinity demonstrates power and authority uniquely.

When I pray, seeking the release of kingdom authority and/or power, I call on the name of Jesus and apply his blood knowing the Holy Spirit and angelic realm is engaged around me. This is a divine mystery. It's impossible to definitively explain the details of how we partner with the Trinity. But I know it's possible. When our positioning and identity in Christ is joined to our dependence on the Father, spoken in the name of Jesus with mindfulness of Holy Spirit power, the supernatural is at hand. The kingdom is at hand.

Today, pray and ask the Lord for an increasing awareness of the gifts of the Holy Spirit.

- Words of Knowledge
- Words of Wisdom
- Gift of Prophecy
- Gift of Faith
- Gift of Healings
- Working of Miracles
- Discerning of Spirits
- Gift of Tongues
- Interpretation of Tongues

But the fruit of the Spirit is love, joy, peace, forbearance, kindness, goodness, faithfulness, gentleness and self-control. Against such things there is no law. Those who belong to Christ Jesus have crucified the flesh with its passions and desires. Since we live by the Spirit, let us keep in step with the Spirit.
GALATIANS 5:22-25

CHAPTER TWELVE

The Power of Our Voice

The tongue has the power of life and death.
PROVERBS 18:21a

"I wasn't heard."

"I was always controlled."

"I felt invisible, insignificant…voiceless."

These are common confessions I hear during a Healing Prayer session. It breaks my heart listening to the pain of those who, for most of their lives, were silenced. Far too many people, from an early age, learn their thoughts and concerns prove worthless to those around them, especially those they trust. They live as unheard and unprotected children and the lies of voicelessness continue to follow them into adult relationships.

However, I smile to myself as I listen. I KNOW what is coming next in prayer. Jesus restores their voice. It's one of the most beautiful healing moments in which I'm allowed to participate.

Here is the truth. Satan is determined to silence humanity. Do you know why?

Our voice is powerful!

He knows when a child of God discovers who they are and whose they are, then connects their identity with their voice, his defeat is certain. Freedom and the abundant life are at hand.

Releasing power and authority of Christ through the Holy Spirit is a matter of confident faith and engaging our voice. Let me state clearly at this point in our Jericho trek, as believers anything that is accomplished through prayer rests under the sovereign hand and will of God. However, when we are living in humble submission through our intimate relationship with God, we are empowered and trusted to move as a benefactor for our Father. And our voice is our strongest weapon of faith.

For though we live in the world, we do not wage war as the world does. The weapons we fight with are not the weapons of the world. On the contrary, they have divine power to demolish strongholds. We demolish arguments and every pretension that sets itself up against the knowledge of God, and we take captive every thought to make it obedient to Christ. And we will be ready to punish every act of disobedience, once your obedience is complete.
2 CORINTHIANS 10:3-6

Our voice is our weapon, and when we combine this weapon with the Sword of the Spirit, speaking the Word, the unseen realm stands up and takes notice.

Let's consider the power of a voice. God spoke the universe into existence. His voice released omnipotent power to the extent that science remains unable to fully decipher the energy, strength, and frequencies that continue to this day resulting from the creation event.

Say what??

*In the beginning God created the heavens and the earth. Now the earth was formless and empty, darkness was over the surface of the deep, and the Spirit of God was hovering over the waters. **And God said**, "Let there be light," and there was light.*
GENESIS 1:1-3

Jesus demonstrates his power and authority through his voice. He spoke and blind eyes were opened, the lame walked, the demonized set free. His example is our model, our possibility. Our voice is a warfare weapon. On the flip side, our voice is also a beautiful bastion of peace.

Death and life are in the power of the tongue: and they that love it shall eat the fruit thereof.
PROVERBS 18:21

I begin every prayer session quoting this verse, explain-

126

ing the depths and strength of our voice when we pray. This verse is legit!

As believers, it's actually possible to set in motion life or death scenarios each time we open our mouth. The gravity of this truth cannot be understated. Our words are empowered and we can wreck our lives, destroy families, crash and burn a marriage, a church, and a child. Or, we can be the one who blesses, releases truth, hope, goodness, and love.

Oh, my friend, please, let us choose life. Stop right now and pray. Confess any sin of your tongue, mouth, or lips. Ask forgiveness, then ask the Lord to place a guard over your mouth and dedicate your mouth to serve only Jesus. It's truly that important. How do I know? Read this scripture.

But I tell you that everyone will have to give account on the day of judgment for every empty word they have spoken.
MATTHEW 12:36

As I mentioned earlier, we are the thermostat in our home and marriage. Comprehending the truth that words are backed up by an unseen realm, we must take our thoughts captive to Christ and speak words that edify, uplift, and carry hope and truth.

Do not let any unwholesome talk come out of your mouths, but only what is helpful for building others up according to their needs, that it may benefit those who listen.
EPHESIANS 4:29

Winning our spouse without a word is our mandate. We won't win our spouse to Jesus through nagging, manipulation, guilt, or shaming them to attend church. 1 Peter 3:1 speaks to this truth.

Whoever desires to love life and see good days, let him keep his tongue from evil and his lips from speaking deceit;
1 PETER 3:10

As kingdom advocates, using our voice to advance the cause of love is our primary mission. And love does not ask us to remain silent, nor be a doormat. Kingdom people are those who possess strength, integrity, character, and wisdom. It's appropriate to set healthy boundaries in our relationships, especially in our marriages. It's appropriate to speak with our spouse regarding any breach of love and respect. And likewise, listen wholeheartedly and respond in love when our spouse speaks about his or her boundaries.

A Child's Voice

Now is the time to rescue back our voice from the darkness. It's time we declare that we are no longer a voiceless victim. Instead, we are children of God, filled with Holy Spirit power, love, and a sound mind.

For God hath not given us the spirit of fear; but of power, and of love, and of a sound mind.
2 TIMOTHY 1:7

Our voice is an extraordinary gift that also carries a great responsibility. Our effectiveness is born from our maturity and character in Christ. Displaying consistent trustworthiness, when wielding our sword without hurting ourselves or others, the Lord then releases greater authority and power into our words.

For me, this was a fantastic time in my learning march. Sometimes I shake my head with wonder when reflecting on the prayers and purposes God trusts me to speak.

I find it astonishing God believes in us and watches with excitement as we advance his purposes on earth. All of heaven leans in with careful attention to our voice as we establish his kingdom on earth. Jericho Marcher, let's make a declaration over our voice right now! Pray out loud:

In the name of Jesus, I exercise my authority according to Luke 10:19 and I renounce every lie that was spoken over me by any authority figure or by myself that my voice didn't matter. I renounce the lies that when I speak no one listens and the lie that my words are powerless or without worth or merit. I break all legal rights of the enemy to silence, drown out, reduce, or diminish my voice and my purposes in the kingdom of God.

Thank you, Jesus, your blood covers any and all

lies I believed that I wasn't worthy to be heard. And now, Jesus, I set a decree (Job 22:28) over myself that my voice is powerful. I declare that I am a voice for the kingdom and that my words are worthy to be heard by all of heaven, hell, and the earth. I also dedicate my voice to truth and the purposes of God. In your powerful name, Jesus, AMEN

And whatever you ask in prayer, you will receive,
if you have faith.
MATTHEW 21:22

Truly, I say to you, whoever says to this mountain, "Be taken up and thrown into the sea," and does not doubt in his heart, but believes that what he says will come to pass, it will be done for him.
MARK 11:23

But he answered, "It is written, 'Man shall not live by bread alone, but by every word that comes from the mouth of God.'"
MATTHEW 4:4

For "Whoever desires to love life and see good days, let him keep his tongue from evil and his lips from speaking deceit."
1 PETER 3:10

DISCERNING GOD'S VOICE

So shall my word be that goes out from my mouth; it shall not return to me empty, but it shall accomplish that which I purpose, and shall succeed in the thing for which I sent it.
ISAIAH 55:11

Everything I've shared about the power and authority of God comes from a place of intimacy with our Father. Our ability to hear the Father speak is key to walking in the power and authority of Christ.

So much of my intimacy journey with God was learning to hear his voice. Intense practice increased my ability to discern his voice from the noise, the voice of the enemy, and my own voice. Time alone in the secret place prepares our spirit to distinguish his whisperings. Our Father will not compete for our attention, our agendas, or our cell phones. However, he waits anxiously to converse and to share his heart with an eager child who is listening.

Let's Pray:

> *Father, I ask you to open my spiritual ears to hear your voice clearly, open my spiritual eyes to see. Increase my discernment to understand the many ways that you speak to me. Shut down all chaos, time stealers, and distractions that work to diminish your voice. I ask to hear you speak to me about myself, others, and everything that you desire to share with me.*

> *Father, let my pursuit of your heart be the motivation in my spirit. I honor you, Father, for you are good and have good for my life. I ask you to tune my heart to yours that I may hear, see, and perceive all that you are speaking and sharing with me. In the name of Jesus, my Savior, AMEN*

God is always speaking, and it is our privilege to turn our heart toward him. When he speaks, everything changes.

My Jericho Journal

DATE: _____

Thou shalt also decree a thing, and it shall be established unto thee: and the light shall shine upon thy ways.
JOB 22:28

    Take this Jericho journal to your secret place. Ask Jesus these questions then listen intently for his reply.

- Jesus, is there any past pain or trauma that has silenced me? (If there is, forgive, bless, and then ask Jesus to reinstate the truth.)

- Jesus, I dedicate my voice to be used by you. What areas of my character need development that I may use my voice with power and authority and without harm?

- Jesus, bless me today to grow in this area of understanding and equipping. What do you want to teach me today about my voice?

_____

_____

_____

_____

_____

_____

_____

_____

_____

_____

_____

YEAR FIVE
Marching Practice

CHAPTER THIRTEEN

Marching Through the Practice Years

Do you not know that in a race all the runners run, but only one gets the prize? Run in such a way as to get the prize.
1 CORINTHIANS 9:24

Four times around the walled city! Woo hoo!!

Intimacy, identity, authority, and power. Do you perceive the rumbling? The once-strong enemy foundations have weakened throughout our truth march. Little does our pre-believer realize that the shaking of their once-prideful veneer, their gods of science, and social constructs looms imminent. The funny thing about reaching the completion of the first four circles is that our spouse may or may not have recognized the powerful changes taking place within.

In the middle of my Jericho March, I began to speak more freely about Jesus to people around me, including my spouse. Ahem, I might have morphed into a freak of nature. A Jesus freak. My identity was unbreakable, and I knew emphatically that no one could shake the truths of my foundation.

Upon this realization, the demons tremble.

Reaching the end of this season, or I should say, reaching the beginning of my blossoming potential, a noticeable shift occurred in our marriage. Dread over my spouse's offhand remarks and his mocking of my faith and criticisms of Christianity ceased. Slowly I found myself sharing crazy God encounters with him. Some he believed. Some he put in a box in his mind. Some of my stories were outside of his grasp. I remember one occasion upon sharing a whacky story, I stated, "You either think I'm crazy or this is real."

He replied, "I don't think you are crazy. I just haven't had that experience. So I'm not sure what I think."

Hmmmmmm.

Each experience I shared became fodder for his mind and spirit with which to contend. Over time, the testimonies I revealed, along with my prayers, as well as the random prayers I prayed aloud in front of him, actually changed him.

THE WILDERNESS YEARS

Be strong and very courageous. Be careful to obey all the law my servant Moses gave you; do not turn from it to the right or to the left, that you may be successful wherever you go.

Keep this Book of the Law always on your lips; meditate on it day and night, so that you may be careful to do everything written in it.

*Then you will be prosperous and successful. Have I not commanded you? Be strong and courageous. **Do not be afraid; do not be discouraged, for the Lord your God will be with you wherever you go**.*

*So Joshua ordered the officers of the people: "Go through the camp and tell the people, 'Get your provisions ready. <u>Three days from now you will cross the Jordan here to go in and **take possession of the land** the Lord your God is giving you for your own.</u>"*
JOSHUA 1:7-11

I've applied considerable meditation to the story of Joshua and the Israelites in the wilderness years. Prior to their wilderness wanderings, they were slaves. Four hundred years of beatings, oppression, and fear. Their daily experience conditioned them into voicelessness, hopelessness, and pain. The taskmasters meticulously developed within the people self-acceptance of life-long servitude.

The day they departed Egypt, they were joyful, yet woefully unprepared to take the Promised Land. And if by some chance they had secured the land, retaining it would be impossible. Although, I do believe that if they'd remained obedient instead of rebelling against God, he would have walked them in under supernatural protection to revel in the milk and honey. How like us, their stubbornness and rebellion created an undesired alternate future. Our rebellion, stubbornness, and our slavery mindset will sidetrack our advancement as well. We stumble into our own slavery born of deception, finding ourselves fighting with the marauders in the land instead of walking in promises and peace.

These unanticipated battles are costly, and they hurt. A lot!

However, our Father redeems everything. Although the Israelites rebelled, God brought them to their senses in the waiting. God's process of redemption and love remains the same for us today. He walks with us, provides, protects, urges us forward even when we are clueless.

Wilderness seasons teach dependence. God displays his faithfulness through the numerous rescues from disaster. He continues to whisper to our hearts, urging us forward despite our weariness and encourages us as we face challenges in our family dynamic.

The wilderness years are our practice years. The Israelites learned how to handle weaponry in the desert. They acquired a battleground acuity through the skirmishes they faced along the way. They battled against the elements, they battled discouragement, and fought against a false promise of returning to the familiarity of slavery was better than the unknown distant promise of God.

The Promised Land scenario has been on repeat for millennia. Generation after generation, it's the same experience within different cultures, different people groups. My hope is that this generation will recognize that living in obedience to our Father is the highest and best for all humanity. I cling to and pray for this possible future.

Yet, I was one of these disobedient children of God. My tour in the badlands of the wilderness proved costly. When I finally stepped out of the badlands and arrived at this place of crossing, I was ready, giddy with anticipation.

For me, circling around Jericho was a walk of preparation, reorienting my faith with truth and the realities of everything that was possible as a child of God. So, in the fifth year I began to practice.

I broke off the lies of impossibility. I stepped into the realm of "all things are possible with God." I became a believing believer. I fully believed the Word and expected to see it come alive before my eyes. My prayer life accelerated. I began to hear the Lord speak to me specifically about others and myself.

I remember that this was the year that I became interested in the prophetic gifts of the Holy Spirit. I would tune in listening for the Lord to speak specifically regarding others and myself. In this season, I intensely prayed the prayer from Ephesians 1.

I keep asking that the God of our Lord Jesus Christ, the glorious Father, may give you the Spirit of wisdom and revelation, so that you may know him better.
EPHESIANS 1:17

I prayed this every single day. If the Apostle Paul prayed this prayer, it was good enough for me. I desired revelation from heaven and the wisdom to know what to do with it. So, I asked the Father to provide. And he did.

I began to discern the spiritual realm around me. I began to perceive the enemy's influence in conversations and situations. I asked God, "Show me what is going on here." I would hear his still small voice immediately and he would clue me in. I would have a "knowing" about situations and people. Somehow information would come to my mind instantly. Information that I couldn't have known. This prophetic gift created amazing healing and hope for others when we prayed together. It was keenly helpful when praying for my husband, son, and daughter.

I commanded enemy bandits out of my house, and I released the angelic to protect. I started serving in my local church in a prophetic capacity, praying for others. And I was simply astonished that God would speak to me his thoughts, his love, and grace regarding others that they would be encouraged and feel his love. This season was a further maturing in my faith, learning to appropriately operate in my prophetic gift, mindful to always edify others and never harm. I'm thankful for the training my church provided in this area.

THE POWER OF BLESSING

Bless those who persecute you; bless and do not curse.
ROMANS 12:14

The power of blessing became a tool I used with growing frequency and experienced remarkable outcomes. Believers struggle with the concept of blessing. Our years of religion instill a false humility that if I bless others, or myself, it's prideful.

Nonsense.

Let's blow that religious mindset out of the water. Jesus demonstrated blessing through the Sermon on the Mount. As disciples, our mandate is to follow the examples of Christ. Blessing is a beautiful gift of love that comes from our heart and voice. And the astonishing truth is this; the heavenly realm responds when we release blessings. When we bless, I know our Father smiles. After all, we are releasing his kingdom.

In this season, I practiced by blessing my physical body. I blessed myself with divine health and healing. I blessed anything and everything that hurt or that needed alignment with truth. I also blessed my husband and his health. I blessed his employer and bosses to discover the value of my husband and ask for him by name to oversee their projects. I blessed my children. My grandchildren. I blessed the server at a restaurant and those who bagged my groceries.

I blessed my dogs.

I said, *I bless you*, to nearly everyone I met. I've only had a few people react weirdly when I bless. Overwhelmingly, most respond with a smile, many bless back or offer a *thank you* in return.

Let me share what a blessing lifestyle looks like in a day in the life of Lynn Donovan.

On a bright January morning, I assisted my daughter

loading her car for her return trip to college for the spring semester. Driving away, I waved then winced. Needle-pricking pain shot through my right eye. For a week, since returning home from a speaking event in Detroit, Michigan, I'd been treating a nasty eye infection without success. And the doctor's prescriptions failed to alleviate the pain. Every morning I woke, my eye stuck closed because of the goop and crud. Geez. Ugh!

Moving from the bright sunlight into the dim garage triggered the irritation. In that precise moment I stood straight up in the garage, fully indignant and angry about this obvious injustice. I'D HAD IT!

I let loose a prayer in the middle of my garage before God and my all my neighbors. Loudly I prayed:

> *In the name of Jesus, I bless my eye into perfect health. I bless it to be free from infection. I bless my eye with divine health. I declare that this infection in my eye MUST GO! I AM A DAUGHTER OF THE KING! In Jesus's name I say GO! You are an illegal illness sent from the devil and I WILL NOT HAVE IT. I command you to leave me right now in the name of my Savior, Jesus. I cover my eye with the blood of Christ. He paid for my healing and I will not waste one drop of blood or settle for less. So right now, in his name and authority, I command this infection to leave my eye. I bless my eye, in Jesus' s name, AMEN*

I threw an absolute fit, waving my arms wildly in the garage as I issued my faith proclamations. I concluded feeling rather proud of my tantrum prayer. Then I turned and walked through the garage door, passed through the laundry room, across the living/dining area, and finally arrived in the kitchen. I stood at the counter deciding what task to tackle next. Surveying the dishes, I absentmindedly reached up and rubbed my infected eye with my finger. A quick back and forth.

As I pulled my finger away, I felt something. There poised on the end of my pointer was an old contact lens.

What?????

I stared as my heart started to beat faster. Astonished, I

uttered, "*It must have been in there since Detroit.*"

I started the giggle, then laugh, then hysterics. Crying and laughing at the same time. My brain worked to catch up with the truth that I was witnessing. God immediately answered my rant/prayer in the garage.

Healed instantly! The infection completely disappeared. Praise Jesus! Hallelujah!

Warriors, this healing kicked off a number of miraculous faith experiences. Since that time God's continued to astonish and delight through answered prayer.

It's a blast living the believer's life!

It's your turn to participate in the miracles of God. Believe and you shall receive.

If you believe, you will receive whatever you ask for in prayer.
MATTHEW 21:22

My Jericho Journal

DATE: _____

Jesus, I desire to participate in the divine. I'm asking to witness the miraculous. Teach me to participate with you in healing miracles. Jesus, demonstrate your blessings in my life. And Jesus, today I am determined to use this amazing gift, the Power of Blessings, to reveal your love and healing to myself and others.

Jesus, I stand in faith upon Matthew 21:22. If you believe, you will receive whatever you ask for in prayer, AMEN

It's time to bless. Write down every blessing you want to release. Bless in the name of Jesus. Have fun!

_____

_____

_____

_____

_____

_____

_____

_____

_____

_____

_____

_____

_____

_____

CHAPTER FOURTEEN

The Power of Peace

And the peace of God, which transcends all understanding, will guard your hearts and your minds in Christ Jesus.
PHILIPPIANS 4:7

I looked across the room at this beautiful woman who just walked in to receive prayer. She was smiling, ready to pray. As I looked at her, the Lord opened my spiritual eyes and I perceived something strange over this woman's head. Just above her head I discerned three swirling, black whirlwinds, each roughly two feet tall. One was positioned over the center of her head. The other two were whirling upward diagonally, with the small ends pointing at her head.

God immediately downloaded to my spirit what was before me. These were spirits of chaos, death, and addiction.

What????

With great love and compassion in my heart, I asked her some questions. "My dear friend, I sense there is so much swirling around you." Careful not to scare or worry her unduly.

Immediately, her countenance broke, she slumped slightly. "Yes, I feel so confused. I'm so upset and beside myself trying to find the answers for my daughter who is an addict."

Whoa!

Immediately I received understanding. Peace had been hijacked from this poor woman's life. She was standing in the midst of extreme torment. Of course, our prayer team went right to work, bringing her freedom from the confusion and fear. The

Holy Spirit revealed to me something interesting through this incident. These three spirits work together and are always present upon those with a serious addiction. And this same cluster will often cling to close family members.

Let the peace of Christ rule in your hearts, since as members of one body you were called to peace. And be thankful.
COLOSSIANS 3:17

I'm of the opinion that evil spirits are capable of creating false joy in the human heart, and they are also able to falsify love. But the one thing the devil CANNOT mimic is peace. For this reason, we endure a relentless assault against all things peaceful.

Chaos is our enemy. The noise of the world created by our fast-paced living, striving, and competing with one another muffles the voice of God and destroys our inner peace. As children of God we are by nature, peaceful. Our souls crave tranquility.

Peacefulness destroys all fear, chaos, anger, striving, and every work of the devil. Peacefulness is our superpower the devil fears. Satan is relentless in his effort to keep us from acquiring the gift of peace in the Holy Spirit. In fact, his anger has flared viscerally knowing you are currently reading this chapter. While I wrote, entire paragraphs would disappear, my documents began to shift in and out of one another, and all of a sudden my laptop battery drained and the screen went dark.

(I found my charging cord. *grin*)

Yep, the devil does not want you to acquire the peace of heaven. Peace opposes everything that is assigned to destroy you and your family.

RELEASE THE PEACE

To whom God would make known what is the riches of the glory of this mystery among the Gentiles; which is Christ in you, the hope of glory.
COLOSSIANS 1:27

I'm of the opinion that a majority of the church is clueless about the power of peace that dwells within. Christ is alive in us. His peace is available at all times. When we release our peace, we are releasing Jesus into our circumstances, we take control of the atmosphere and the devil must bow the knee to Christ.

Let me share an example of how to release peace.

Just yesterday I was standing in the return line at Walmart. The tension was so thick among those in line, you could cut it with a knife. A single cashier worked desperately to serve two different lines of customers. Yikes. I had such compassion for her. People began grumbling, tempers rose.

I made my way through my return thankful the grumbling hadn't escalated into shouting. Leaving the returns desk, I joined my husband who was standing in a store checkout lane. As soon as I stepped into line, I began to sense a tension-filled weirdness rise all over the store. In our lane, three customers ahead, the cashier and an older man, who was making an effort to pay, began to squawk back and forth. I could feel a dark presence increase in the spiritual realm. Then, as if on cue, a small boy sitting in a cart in front of us let loose three high-pitched screams. The entire store front turned to look. Right on the heels of our ears bleeding, two women began yelling and cussing at the poor cashier working on their order in the next lane.

Sheesh!

I looked back at the return line. My friend, I was certain a fistfight was imminent. I looked at Mike and said, "The atmosphere is throbbing with conflict and anger." He knew what was coming. (Poor guy)

I started walking back and forth right there in the checkout lanes. I began to pray aloud, in a lower-than- normal volume, but loud enough for the devils to hear me.

> *"In the name of Jesus, I take authority over this store. I command these spirits of conflict, witchcraft, fighting spirits, and all spirits of anger to STAND DOWN NOW. In Jesus's name. I release my peace that comes from my Father in heaven into this store. I release the peace of Jesus that I carry into all of these people and these situations. In Jesus's powerful name, AMEN*

I continued to walk back and forth, praying in tongues. I know I looked like a crazy lady and Mike was likely rolling his eyes, but every angry situation began to resolve and calm down. Mike continued with our checkout. I noticed the store manager send another employee to the returns desk. The conflicts among the employees and the customers dissipated.

We gathered our bags and left the store. I was relieved there wasn't a fight in the lobby. Thank you, Jesus!

For several years now, I exercise my authority over our home. I command anything not of God to depart and release peace, joy, truth, and love into our home. I bless my husband, our dogs, with peace. Our home is a peaceful place. I wasn't aware of the extent of the peaceful atmosphere resting in our home until a girlfriend who visits a couple times a year said, "I love to visit you. And your home. It's just so peaceful."

Wow, she discerns the peace of Jesus.

PEACE CHALLENGE

But the fruit of the Spirit is love, joy, peace, forbearance, kindness, goodness, faithfulness, gentleness, and self-control.
GALATIANS 5:22-23

It's time for the sons and daughters of God to step up and release what we carry. If you aren't walking in peace, start now to remove things that cause strife, such as mindless, crass, over-sexualized, violent television programing, fast from social media and news broadcasts. Begin to bless your home every day aloud with peace.

Bless yourself first with peace. Bless your kids as you drive them to school. Bless your spouse with peace before they start their workday. Bless your mind with peace. Bless your body with peace. Bless your church with peace.

This absolutely works, I promise. So, here is the challenge, for the next 30 days read passages about peace, joy, and becoming an overcomer. Start each day by speaking aloud a peace blessing over your home, children, spouse, marriage, work, etc. Always bless in the name of Jesus. Peace will come and it begins with you.

If you don't take much from the book, please take this challenge with you. If we collectively, as the believing Church of Jesus Christ, walked in peace together on a single day, all the works of the devil would be destroyed, and the world would change forever.

This is the power of peace of Jesus Christ. And this peace is ours to give away.

Freely you have received; freely give.
MATTHEW 10:8b

My Jericho Journal

DATE: _____

    Read and reflect: Tranquility, calm, serenity, quiet, placidity, rest, comfort, contentment, peacefulness, relaxation, repose, respite, restfulness, stillness, harmony, placidness, relief, freedom from interference.

    How do you feel when you read this list?

    Peace is our divine, natural atmosphere because we are eternal beings. It is our Father's world and our soul longs to live in tranquility, unity, and peaceful love.

    When we are seated in heavenly realms with Christ, it's out of this positioning that we become powerful intercessors. Pray for discernment, wisdom, and revelation to release the peace you carry inside into your world.

    How are you going to release the peace of Jesus?

_____

_____

_____

_____

_____

_____

_____

_____

_____

_____

_____

_____

CHAPTER FIFTEEN

The Power of Love

*Jesus replied: "'Love the Lord your God with all your heart and
with all your soul and with all your mind.' This is the first and
greatest commandment. And the second is like it:
'Love your neighbor as yourself.'"*
MATTHEW 22:37-39

I'm of the belief that upon arriving at heaven's gate, Jesus
will look into our eyes and ask a single question, "Did you learn
to love?"

Jesus commands us to love God and love people. Loving
God is easy. People, well, not so much.

I'll be vulnerable here. There are many people that I meet
who love easily. They always choose to notice the best in others.
It's not that easy for me. Walking into adulthood, I carried with
me beliefs that no one was reliable or trustworthy and that I was
utterly on my own. No one had my back. Including God.

Of course, these were lies, but I lived them out as truth
for many years. Unwinding these false beliefs required years
of God relentlessly loving me until over time, my heart finally
cracked open. His love filled me to the point that I could love
with authenticity and learn to trust people. Releasing my fears of
abandonment and distrust felt as though I removed a giant back-
pack from my shoulders. And once gone, I became free to dream
with God. I was freed up to imagine the impossible and discover
gifts and abilities I didn't know I already possessed. And loving
people became easier.

My dear warrior, our entire journey upon this planet is a quest to learn to love. Love is an easy word; however, it's been hijacked, perverted, and applied to numerous ideologies. Our assignment for this life is to love people from the source, our heavenly Father. We can't fail to get this one right.

Every day we make a thousand choices. With each choice, we walk down one of two paths, love or fear. Oh, let us choose bravely and walk in love.

As I write this book, I'm older now and have walked with Jesus for over 50 years. I've reflected on decades of life choices and the consequences of choosing fear over love. From my vantage point, the choice of love is always the best course with a better result than living in a false sense of security that fear perpetuates.

Choosing love is a risk. We risk our heart. We risk pain and rejection. However, living wholeheartedly far and away exceeds the risk.

In every decision where I chose to love over bowing to fear, contributed to my refining process. When I risked loving but I was met by disappointment and pain because love wasn't returned, Jesus arrived with gold from heaven and filled the cracks of my broken heart. If you could picture my heart today, it is whole, but a closer view reflects tiny golden-white-light lines where the pieces of my brokenness were gathered together. All the heart-pieces rescued back from childhood pain, a divorce, an unexpected move, the loss of what I desired from my marriage.

Our heart is made whole by Christ's love, redemption, and healing. Our hearts become a beautiful recreation of his design. A recreated heart overflows with empathy, compassion, and depth of understanding as well as a wealth of patience. This is the heart of God.

I will give you a new heart and put a new spirit in you; I will remove from you your heart of stone and give you a heart of flesh.
EZEKIEL 36:26

Warrior, love heals all trauma. One touch of the Savior's love and a difficult upbringing, abuse, disappointment, fears, and all failures of the past are redeemed. The Redeemer seals love and peace over our pain which silences the lies of the devil. He is our blessing. He is our peace. He is love.

Everything the enemy has used to hurt and destroy you, God will redeem. And in the Kingdom of God, the evil meant to kill you will become the very thing that God will use within you to rescue and bring healing to others. Your pain becomes your superpower. Your woundedness becomes your peace. Your destruction is the birthplace of a love that the demons cannot touch.

Love redeems our past, establishes our present, is our future and our children's legacy.

Choose love and live strong.

And now these three remain: faith, hope and love. But the greatest of these is love.
1 CORINTHIANS 13:13

My Jericho Journal

DATE: _____

Take time to ask Father to speak love and healing into your heart. Ask him to help you "feel" his love. Pray about the broken areas of your heart and ask Jesus to call your heart together and pour his healing, crimson-golden love over the cracks. Ask Jesus to touch and heal every soul wound.

Ask the Lord how your life's experiences should become a ministry. Ask him to help you use your past hurt and pain to rescue others. Ask him to open doors for ministry in your area of power and strength.

_____

_____

_____

_____

_____

_____

_____

_____

_____

_____

_____

_____

_____

Year Six
Fire
Marchers

Fire of God
and Refiner's Fire

*Jesus replied: "Love the Lord your God with all your heart and
with all your soul and with all your mind." This is the first and
greatest commandment. And the second is like it: "Love your
neighbor as yourself."*
MATTHEW 22:37-39

It happened! The walls cracked in an indefinable moment in the middle of this year in my smith circumference. I
noticed a subtle change in my husband. His hard opinions regarding all things Christian softened. His face softened, I spotted
ongoing kindness and gentleness in his smile. To my surprised
delight, we actually exchanged random moments of humor over
faith. When I dragged home yet another Mylar balloon from my
morning walk-n-pray, lighthearted conversations followed over
the implied message from God. A tangible joy became a regular
presence in our home. This man looked like the same guy I'd
married more than 27 years ago, yet different.

In the middle of year six of this epic march, I felt as though
my faith life supercharged. My classroom time with Rabbi Jesus
was paying off. I found myself on the super-fast track of spiritual
development. My life-changing encounter in worship six years
previous occurred in my early fifties. God determined to make
up for lost time. My ever-increasing hunger to uncover and live
in growing intimacy with the Father compelled me forward.

A stack of books piled high on the table in my prayer room. I continually listened to audio books in the car and watched YouTube videos. I searched out lessons from pastors and teachers who offered insight into healing, deliverance, intercession, the prophetic, the goodness of God, God's love, etc. You get the picture. I connected with other believers who were in a similar place in their faith walk, meeting with them often as we excitedly compared notes.

It was in this season that I joined my local church's healing prayer team. This was eye opening and amazing. I remember a session in which a young woman arrived for prayer. She clearly stated she wasn't a believer but open to spirituality. What a privilege to share the love and healing of Jesus with her. Then I humbly led her in prayer to receive Jesus as her Savior. We prayed healing into her childhood wounding; Jesus proved again his power and love in her life. Nearing the end of the session she looked to me and said, "What are these gold things spinning about my head?" Her hands spun around in tight circles near her ears.

Clearly, she was encountering something in the spiritual realm. Warrior, in that prayer room, we caught a glimpse of God that freaked us out in such a good way. Gold dust began to appear on her clothing. First across her stomach and then down her left leg.

Say what???

I can't explain things like this. But the young woman, myself and my prayer assistant, well, the three of us in that room were touched by the fantastic love and the miraculous display of God's glory. We will never be the same.

In fact, this isn't the only time gold dust has appeared. Gold dust, feathers, messages in the clouds—these unique manifestations of the kingdom of God became a somewhat regular occurrence in the weirdest of times and in strange places. Along with these tiny love notes, as I've come to call them, I've heard heavenly music, but the best part of this year became the increasing awareness of God's abiding Presence in me and around me.

My prophetic ability increased significantly and so did my authority over the demonic in year six. The fire of God burned in my bones!

In year six, prompted by the Holy Spirit, I prayed daily for healing in my body in every area. I blessed myself, aloud, with divine health. And as of the writing of this book, I'm living well, blessed with divine health, and I'm medication free at age 60. Praise Jesus!

This was a year of wonder and a year of continued growth. Everything I'd practiced, gained, and asked of God in the past four years was engaged.

This was also a year of significant assaults.

THE REFINER'S FIRE

In all this you greatly rejoice, though now for a little while you may have had to suffer grief in all kinds of trials. These have come so that the proven genuineness of your faith—of greater worth than gold, which perishes even though refined by fire—may result in praise, glory and honor when Jesus Christ is revealed.
1 PETER 1:6-7

The assaults upon my faith came in the form of accusation in year six. The devil was enraged by my prayers and hell bent to distract and hurt me.

As I mentioned earlier in the book, offense is one of the devil's greatest weapons. Year six brought with it three different accusations from women who were offended with me.

For more than a decade I've lived somewhat in the public eye. I've gained experience over the years, learning how to navigate and handle those who disagree with my writing. Pushback will arrive from those who merely want to make noise and don't take the time to get to know my heart. They are quick to condemn and then move on.

However, this year the accusations came from other believers that I knew personally and held in trusted relationships. The first came from a wounded woman who attended my local church who made an accusation behind my back. After many tears, a ton of prayer and conversations with Jesus, the truth was made known and I was exonerated, but the pain was real. The pain was deep.

The enemy delights to turn believers against one another

to destroy us from within. If we would only use the biblical model of Matthew 18 to resolve church issues, we would be a united church that no one could destroy.

Oy vey.

This was followed by two more issues that arrived in my online ministry, by trusted friends and a team member. I'll be forthright here. At times I felt as though the blows would keep me down and out of the game.

The accusations were personal, hurtful, and untrue. And what was truly frustrating was that I was judged and never offered a chance to explain or ask what happened. This kind of cowardice among believers is one of the many reasons our unbelieving spouses dislike religion. Explaining all this to my husband was difficult.

I spent hours and hours in prayer. I asked the Lord a lot of questions. I searched myself to understand my sin or where I failed or didn't line up with scripture. It was a humbling process. It was a necessary process. In fact, my wholehearted, utter dependence on God was birthed from this season of tears.

In the pain, we gain and learn much. For me, the lessons of complete dependence on God kept my pride in check. In this pain I embraced the absolute truth—I am wholly dependent upon God for protection. I am wholly dependent upon God for any and all victories. My ego was crushed under the blows and I am better for it today.

Warriors, prepare to experience pushback in this journey. Accusation from the brethren isn't easy. But our good Father always points us to truth, redeems and guides us through. Press on. His love is worthy of all our sacrifice.

It was a tough year, but triumphs by far outweighed the pain.

Finally, in year six, I stepped into a new level of faith experience with the Lord. This was the year our family experienced significant and multiple financial breakthroughs in the Courts of Heaven.

The Courts of Heaven played a substantial role in the final battle in year seven. In the next chapter let's learn about the kingdom courts and how we access this amazing prayer place to receive justice and rulings from heaven.

My Jericho Journal

DATE: _____

    Ask the Lord to grant you fire to burn down enemy strongholds.

    Pray and ask the Lord to reveal any areas of your life that require submission. Ask for protection from all word curses and all accusations. Ask the Lord to bless you and place a cover over your mouth, lips, and tongue with the wisdom of his love.

_____

_____

_____

_____

_____

_____

_____

_____

_____

_____

_____

_____

_____

_____

_____

_____

_____

CHAPTER SEVENTEEN

Courts of Heaven

God presides over heaven's court; he pronounces judgment on the heavenly beings.
PSALM 81:2

I'm convinced that believers today are living in one of the most unique and powerful dispensations of God's timeline. It appears to me we are experiencing a spiritual shift of monumental importance and opportunity. Throughout recorded history, God releases humanity into new seasons of great change such as The Great Reformation, First and Second Great Awakenings, and the Azusa Street Revival, to name a few.

I wholeheartedly believe the Church is smack in the middle of a major transition, which began roughly around the start of the 21st century. The people of God are departing from a slave mentality and becoming sons and daughters. Collectively, the "Church Age" is evolving into what I term "The Kingdom Age."

I loved my time in the church age. I acquired the core foundations of loving God and loving people and the Word was preached and became the bedrock of my life. But this new season of Kingdom living and Kingdom advancement, well, it's utterly thrilling.

The Kingdom Age brings with it previously unknown revelation and also launches the sons and daughters of God into a modern Acts Two Church. Hallelujah! I'm convinced we are watching this unfold before our very eyes. As I've shared earlier, I was an ordinary believer in an ordinary church. Yet, the Father went to great lengths to move me out of mediocre faith into a faith that is filled with power and authority through our Savior, Jesus Christ.

Kingdom Warrior, by merely reading this book, you are inducted into this powerful new season.

You are welcome!

In year six of my marching, the Lord revealed this fascinating new avenue of prayer, the Courts of Heaven. I investigated the teaching that surrounds this new revelation. I searched out the biblical underpinnings for what I was learning. And then one day, I found myself in a courtroom in heaven. And what resulted from that visit was truly astounding.

It's imperative I lay out the foundations of this new prayer approach because you will use this new tool in the final battle for your spouse's salvation. Stepping into the Courts of Heaven is imperative to initiate tearing down the strongholds that surround our pre-believer's heart.

THE FOUNDATION OF HEAVEN'S COURTS

*But you have come to Mount Zion, to the city of the living God, the heavenly Jerusalem. You have come to thousands upon thousands of angels in joyful assembly, to the church of the firstborn, whose names are written in heaven. You have come to **God, the Judge of all**, to the spirits of the righteous made perfect, to Jesus the mediator of a new covenant, and to the sprinkled blood that speaks a better word than the blood of Abel.*
HEBREWS 12:22–2

Search the Word and you'll discover numerous passages containing legal language as well as references to courts, justice, thrones, judges, etc. Let's consider a number of passages that were tremendously helpful in my understanding.

*Let us then **approach God's throne of grace** with confidence, so that we may receive mercy and find grace to help us in our time of need.*
HEBREWS 4:16

For the accuser of our brothers and sisters, who accuses them before our God day and night, has been hurled down.
REVELATION 12:10

*And I saw a **great white throne**, and him that sat on it, from whose face the earth and the heaven fled away; and there was found no place for them. And I saw the dead, small and great, stand before God; and **the books were opened**: and another book was opened, which is the book of life: and the dead were **judged out of those things which were written in the books**, according to their works.*
REVELATION 20:11-12

These passages offered me a new paradigm to approaching God in prayer. Up until this time, I've always approached the Lord as Father, and also as my friend, but in this new season of prayer, the Lord invited me to approach him as the Righteous Judge. Jesus became my advocate and the Holy Spirit and angels were the verdict/decree enforcers.

*My dear children, I write this to you so that you will not sin. But if anybody does sin, we have an **advocate** with the Father—*
Jesus Christ, the Righteous One.
1 JOHN 2:1

I attended a meeting in the sixth year which unpacked the scripture references to the Courts of heaven, specifically a court of accusation. In this courtroom, the children of God are welcomed to petition the Judge, who by the way is also our Father. In this court, we seek justice and a resulting ruling, revoking legal claims the enemy has levied against us.

Satan, the accuser, is a legalist. He gains authority from our misspoken words, emotional wounds and the lies we believe. Let me share an example.

Careless words I toss around without much thought such as, *He will never believe. My husband is an atheist. My marriage is a disappointment, etc.* The enemy snatches up my words, looking to gain any and every avenue to legally enforce them. He IS the accuser of the brethren.

As a representative of the kingdom, when words leave our tongue, they are legal directives. The spiritual realm will act upon our dictates, both angelic and demonic. In this scenario, my words of accusation granted the enemy legal rights to enforce negative words against my husband. MY OWN WORDS created spiritual chains, which bound him to old atheistic belief patterns. I was astonished to uncover the far-reaching effects of my words. Yet, right there in the Bible I discovered how the kingdom functions as a legal system. The sheer number of supporting scriptures left little doubt in my mind. Consider this passage:

> *But I say unto you, That every idle word that men shall speak,*
> *they shall give account thereof in the day of judgment.*
> MATTHEW 12:36

This verse came screaming home into my reality. My own words were legal rights for the enemy to bind and delay my husband's passage from bondage into freedom. Gulp!

Possessing this new revelation about the courts of heaven, the next morning I determined to pray, seeking justice from God, the judge of all, in his court of accusation.

A Morning in Court

Let us therefore come boldly to the throne of grace, that we may
obtain mercy and find grace to help in time of need.
HEBREWS 4:16

I began praying, following the simple example the speaker demonstrated in the meeting the prior evening. I closed my eyes and I asked the Lord's permission to enter his courtroom. Permission granted. I then asked for Jesus, my advocate, and the Holy Spirit to accompany me. I perceived in my mind large wooden double doors. I asked for the blood of Jesus to cover the court and my entry. I visualized the blood of Christ applied over the frame of the doors.

The doors opened inward. The three of us stepped forward and up to a long table with a menorah lampstand on the end. I thanked the Lord and then asked the books be opened. In my mind a large book lay open on the table before us. Then I asked my accuser to present himself and make his accusations known to the court. Immediately, at the other end of the table, a swirling black whirlwind appeared.

Wow.

I pictured to my left an enormous wooden bench or throne. The bench was tall, stretching up beyond my vision. I couldn't see the Judge, but I knew the Lord was seated there, eager to listen. I discerned his voice and court was in session.

I prayed, asking the accuser to make known the accusations against me.

Through what I learned the night before, I knew not to argue about any accusation the accuser levied. My role was to repent and ask forgiveness, then ask Jesus to cover the sins under his blood.

Settle matters quickly with your adversary who is taking you to court.
MATTHEW 5:25a

Immediately upon asking, a list of accusations came forth. I could hear words such as liar, murderer, past sexual sins, selfishness, and pride. Whoa…I wanted to argue about all of these. Surely, I'm not that? But Jesus quickly quieted me with one sentence, "Lynn, you can murder a person's character with your words."

Ouch.

So, no matter the accusations, I repented. I asked for forgiveness and received the covering of the blood. I prayed, receiving Christ's forgiveness with humility and thanksgiving. Then I asked to reveal accusations the enemy held against my husband and children through words I'd carelessly spoken in the past.

My friend, we have tremendous authority in the spiritual realm over our immediate family members based upon 1 Corinthians 7:14. Our petitions are super powered because of the trust God has placed in those of us who are married to pre-believers. Our faith sanctifies and covers our family. Also, because much of the spiritual-legal realm is based upon God's structure of family, a believing mother and wife exercises great influence and authority over children and spouse.

At this point in prayer, I began to hear accusations where the enemy pounced on private conversations, spoken only to my husband. I bemoaned to my husband about certain choices my children had made, and I whined about their perceived mistakes. I thought these conversations were private, but the enemy is always lurking, waiting to write down every cruel, unkind, or accusatory word. Each became a binding cord of the devil. He held my husband and children in bondage through the very words I spoke in haste, anger, selfishness, and stupidity.

I grieved over the words. I was sick over what I'd said because the full impact of understanding struck my heart. I've chained those I love the most, and somehow denied or delayed their progress toward their kingdom destiny. I cried. I prayed. I repented. I listened. And I confessed. It took nearly two hours. And a lot of Kleenex.

Finally, I asked again, "Are there any more accusations against me or my family?"

Silence.

Next, the Father handed down four scrolls from his tall, wooden bench. I discerned I was receiving a scroll for each of my immediate family members: husband, son, daughter, and myself. I also sensed they contained verdicts regarding our finances, which was interesting because I hadn't approached the court with a specific financial request.

I thanked the Lord for his justice and forgiveness. I thanked Jesus for helping me through and I asked the Holy Spirit and my angels to fulfill what was written in the scrolls.

Courtroom Justice

Do not take revenge, my dear friends, but leave room for God's wrath, for it is written: "It is mine to avenge;
I will repay," says the Lord.
ROMANS 12:19

Later that day, that very day, I was in my prayer room and my husband walked in. "You won't believe it, but my boss asked me to apply for a new position in the company. It sounds like a fantastic opportunity."

I looked at him, stunned. Then congratulated him as a knowing smile lifted the corners of my lips. I KNEW God initiated this promotion opportunity.

I kid you not, the following week my daughter phoned me from college. "Mom," she enthusiastically rushed on, "I just received a reply from Purdue University." Caitie had applied for a master's degree and hoped to be accepted for the fall semester.

"Mom, I was accepted, and not only that, they are offering me a full scholarship and will pay me to teach. That covers all of my living expenses." Her scholarship and tuition were valued at $120,000. Gulp!

I nearly dropped the phone with shock. I laughed with her. I cried. I hung up the phone and I PRAISED! There was something to this courtroom thing. In this season of discovery, it became apparent through legalities the enemy will delay, detain, and bind up blessings and freedoms through our words.

I caution you, the Lord's heavenly court is never about money or selfish ambition. I went into the court to seek release from careless words. Also, I never enter the court asking for justice against another person. I only want justice against the accuser of the brethren. Bringing Satan to justice changes lives, releases divine callings and holy destinies.

This was my first experience in the courtroom. But I began to regularly visit the court. Always with reverence, anxious to offer repentance and seek forgiveness.

In year six, I began to frequent the court seeking justice. I asked for rulings and verdicts of recompense against demonic attacks against the state of California and finally for America. I entered the courts seeking to throw down all incantations of evil and witchcraft released over our valley where I live. I always enter the courtroom with Jesus, the Holy Spirit, and angels and by the prompting of the Father. I ask permission to enter and always look for the blood covering. I position myself before the Lord with humility and thanksgiving as a daughter of the King. It's always the same protocols.

Finally, and this is important, I only enter into the court and make petitions with the full assurance of God's invitation and instruction. Taking on something not within our authority can release unwanted and painful repercussions. It's only with a specific mandate by God, that I challenge anything. Effective warfare is accomplished when we are fully submitted and walking in the authority and assignment given by God.

DESTROYING PRINCIPALITIES

For we wrestle not against flesh and blood, but against principalities, against powers, against the rulers of the darkness of this world, against spiritual wickedness in high places.
EPHESIANS 6:12

In late September in southern California the daytime temperatures run HOT. Really hot. The landscape is brown and walking among the vineyards requires a pre-dawn start. One particular morning, I was prayer-walking and the landscape reflected the weariness of the heat. The California drought was stretching into year eight with no end in sight. At the time, our drought conditions were broadcast regularly on all the national news networks. And personally, our water bill significantly increased to rival that of a car payment. Grrrrr.

My soul longed to catch sight of any wild greenery while I walked. Southern California was groaning under the relentless heat and serious lack of rain. I walked along and began to pray, asking God to open the heavens and send rain. And at that precise moment God responded, "Lynn, there is a principality sitting on a throne over Los Angeles that is blocking the rain. I want you to put on your royal robes, kick that thing off, and then sit on the throne."

Whoa. Immediately, I determined to follow the Lord's instruction. In my mind, in the spirit realm, I saw myself donning a beautiful, flowing, regal robe of deep red with an ermine-type collar. A large and heavy crown was upon my head and my hair was coifed in an updo. Weird and cool at the same time. Then somehow, I held a scepter in my right hand. Double whoa!

A throne floating in the sky above Los Angeles appeared. I simply said, "Be gone," to the dark thing sitting there. It slithered away like it was on fire. I sat down. God spoke again, "Lynn, now speak to the clouds of the North, command them to come down to southern California. Command the jet stream to push down in an arc to bring the clouds. Then speak to the storehouses of rain and snow in heaven to be opened and release generously upon the land."

Understand, in the natural, I'm still walking and praying OUT LOUD with such a loud voice of authority, I surprised myself. As I began to speak these decrees, a specific scripture came to mind.

"Now pick up the other arrows," said Elisha. He picked them up.

*Then he said to the king of Israel, "**Strike the ground**."*

The king struck the ground three times and then quit.

The Holy Man became angry with him: "Why didn't you hit the ground five or six times? Then you would beat Aram until he was finished. As it is, you'll defeat him three times only."
2 KINGS 13:18-19

The king in this story lacked persistence. And the Holy Spirit was revealing to me I was to persistently pray and to ask for storm, after storm, after storm, after storm, after storm, until I'd exhausted the breath in my lungs.

I began to pray. I spoke to the clouds in the North. I commanded the jet stream to arc. I called forth the clouds then opened the storehouses and finally placed a demand on all of heaven to send forth storm, after storm, after storm, after storm, after storm...... I repeated those two words until I couldn't utter another storm. I had no idea how many storms I released. And in fact, until the rain began a few months later, I'd tucked this particular experience away in my heart.

However, the rain came. It began in January. The successive storms brought relief to our entire state. The snow pack replenished. The reservoirs filled. The land turned green and the hills filled with flowers. A number of stunning anomalies occurred in the spring months which were a direct result of plentiful rain. Millions of painted lady butterflies filled the skies the entire month of May. This is a phenomenon only possible due to the amount of rainfall. It was glorious to watch a hundred flit by in only minutes. And perhaps you caught the news stories about thousands upon thousands of people visiting the wild orange poppy fields near our home. Millions upon millions of these wildflowers decorated the once-brown hills of southern California. Google some of the photos. Our God is beautiful.

An eight-year drought was declared OVER!

Now, did I really pray this into reality? I don't know. It rains every spring in Southern California, but this was record breaking amounts of rain. Also, I'm aware other faithful prayer warriors were petitioning for rain as well. But, is it possible that ordinary believers who truly walk in such authority can affect the weather?

Oh, I do hope so!

By the way, total rainfall for the year was a whopping 19.87 inches. The prior year was a mere 4.72.

God is good!

Approach
the Throne of Grace

The one who does what is sinful is of the devil, because the devil has been sinning from the beginning. The reason the Son of God appeared was to destroy the devil's work.

1 JOHN 3:8

It's glory to partner with God to destroy the work of the devil!

If praying in the Courts of Heaven is a new concept for you, search the Word and conduct your own study. Ask the Lord to lead you. The first time I entered the courtroom, I felt uncertain about the process. I simply asked Jesus to help me and forgive me if I didn't know the protocols or didn't do something right. I asked he cover any mistakes I might make.

There is life-changing justice to be gained before the Lord's court. Powerful edicts are issued and our words are no longer held against us or those we love.

God is releasing new strategies and blueprints to advance his purposes through his children. The court of heaven is an essential strategy to place into our tool belt.

And they overcame him by the blood of the Lamb,
and by the word of their testimony;
and they loved not their lives unto the death.
REVELATION 12:11

# My Jericho Journal

DATE:

It's your turn. Ask Jesus, your Advocate, to walk with you into the Court of Accusation. Walk through the process I described and be attentive to what you hear and see in your prayer time. Forgive yourself, forgive others, and release your family and yourself into the destinies recorded in our books before time began.

Your eyes saw my unformed body; all the days ordained for me were written in your book before one of them came to be.
PSALM 139:16

The War March
& the Glory Realm

Chapter Eighteen

The Promise

Jesus replied: "Love the Lord your God with all your heart and with all your soul and with all your mind." This is the first and greatest commandment. And the second is like it: "Love your neighbor as yourself."
MATTHEW 22:37-39

We are nearing the end of the march. Only one year remains. Each lesson from the years trudging around the walled city are leading to this single heroic appointment.

I stepped into the final year of my march unaware I'd been traversing the path around my husband for nearly seven years. I was oblivious my initial encounter with the Lord in 2012 at Bethel became the antithesis for this spirit-filled journey. It wasn't until supernatural events decreed by God began to take place in rapid succession that I was able to comprehend the significance of the past six years. And this journey around my husband, well it turns out it never was about my husband. The circles around Jericho became my transformation journey.

God knows what he's doing. The difficulties in my married life paled, irrelevant and powerless in the light and love of Christ Jesus. I'll make you a promise. God is extending an invitation for you to springboard off my testimony into a life-transformation journey of your own.

The final year is spectacular so let's jump into the adventure of year seven with expectation. The years of study, the relentless practice and application, humble surrender, and the development of Godly character culminate into one final epic battle.

However, Kingdom Marcher, we aren't really facing one single battle. In fact, I discovered in the seventh year of my march the war for my husband's heart and salvation began with my very first step of my journey—the step into intimacy.

Think about it. I turned to the Lord to fulfill the deepest needs of my heart and gained life-changing intimacy. I released my husband from unrealistic expectations, discovering God fulfilled, then surpassed all my needs, wants, and desires. Wow, what a revelation. With every passing year, new lessons adjusted my expectations for my marriage and spouse.

The war for the soul of our marriage and for the heart of my husband began with my very first step into intimacy. I never perceived I was at war. I was merely stepping into my original design, a child of God. And from a place of PEACE, the battles raged against the enemies of God and not against my husband.

And although I faced a final showdown in year seven, I gained enormous territory through living every day in the presence of the King.

Wow, what a beautiful surprise. A gift of profound grace. God IS JUST THAT GOOD!

GLIMPSES OF GLORY

He that dwelleth in the secret place of the most High shall abide under the shadow of the Almighty.
PSALM 91:1

As year six drew to a close, the Father and I lived in a moment-upon-moment intimacy. Christ in me, the hope of glory is my truth.

Through intimacy with the Lord, his voice was familiar and constant in my life. I sensed his ever-present love. I spoke with God all day long. Our relationship mandated full transparency and my utter dependence rested upon his wisdom and direction. I continued to hunger for increased level of intimacy and experience that ultimately led to greater revelation, fun, hilarious, and astonishing adventures with the king.

On a warm summer morning in the waning of year six, while walking and praying down a country road, I stepped into the chamber of the Father. For a number of months leading up to this encounter, I'd applied myself to pray and visualize myself seated at the feet of Father in his private chamber. I would pray and ask for entry and then seat myself at his feet. I would see his feet. I would liken his skin's appearance to a shimmery, light-filled color fluctuating between light blue tinged with greens, pinks, golds, and white. It was astonishingly beautiful and was alive with color and glistening movement. Is it no wonder we are delighted by bright and sparkly things?

I joined the Father to just…be. In his presence is perfect peace. I would often feel his hand upon my bowed head as I sat quietly. Seldom did we pass words to one another. It was pure contentment and pleasure to be in one another's presence. I loved on him and him on me.

So, back to this specific morning. I entered into the chamber and was seated on the floor. The chamber walls appeared carved of dark gray stone, such as a cave, and a brilliant light shone down, emanating from God. I sat in his presence in contented prayer.

Then suddenly to my great surprise, something different began to unfold. God stood up. He took me by the right hand and said, "Let me show you what you have built." I didn't understand what he meant but I stood.

We turned and faced the back wall of the chamber as he held my hand. The giant walled chamber began to thunder. The entire back wall lurched open and slowly rumbled to the left. I stood hand-in-hand with the Father, feeling like a nine-year-old girl. (There is something to child-like faith I'm still grasping to comprehend.)

The chamber wall completely disappeared, and there in the distance, under brilliant light, were two twin mountain peaks. It was stunning. Beautiful and full of life. The plants and animals on the hills were numerous. I took in the landscape whose sheer beauty filled my heart, and I experienced an aspect of joy that was unfamiliar but utterly holy. My eyes darted around at all the beauty. Then I drew my focus to what was directly before me.

About fifteen steps out of the chamber was a walled city. It was a small city, constructed ornately and intertwined with flora and fauna. Atop the walls, I viewed the extraordinary architecture of water troughs and iron waterspouts. Crystal blue gurgling water flowed continuously throughout the city through these troughs that were intertwined with brilliant pink flowers growing everywhere throughout the dwellings.

This vision overwhelmed me as I held the Father's hand. I glanced away from the water troughs and saw standing by the exterior wall Jesus, smiling at me. When I saw his smile, I sensed the Father was telling me,

This is your dwelling. This IS your home!

This is the dwelling place Jesus went to prepare for me. Jesus's sacrifice created this place for me. And in that moment, a knowing came to my mind as the Father smiled down into my wide eyes.

Jesus prepared this place for me. But I built it.

Revelation filled my heart as the Lord granted me comprehension this home of spectacular beauty is my creation, built with every prayer I uttered on earth. I created this mansion with every breath I prayed for others, each time I served another person, every time I chose calling over comfort and gave to others, I was laying a brick, a fountain within my eternal, heavenly home.

My emotions surged as the implications of my earthly life became reality in the heavens. Every personal sacrifice I made on earth was building my dwelling in the eternal kingdom.

I was astonished, completely overwhelmed by the implications pouring into my mind. I was bawling in the natural as I continued to walk the path through the vineyards. I snot-cried the remainder of my walk. My body walked, but my dear friend, I'm convinced in that moment, my spirit was with God and he was providing a gift of extravagant proportions, the revealing of a lifetime of faith. I witnessed the heavenly reward awaiting all saints upon our passing into the eternal kingdom.

The Father took a step from the edge of the chamber toward Jesus. I walked in tandem. And I sensed a moment of paternal humor pass between the Father and Son. Then I understood. My Father was proud of me. And the Father and Jesus were enjoying my wide-eyed wonder. They exchanged a chuckle and nodded their approval of my ideas, my creation.

Then a knowing arrived in my mind. It was my idea to plumb Living Water throughout the entire place. And this was a new idea, something many other children hadn't considered for their dwelling. We were all smiles; Father and Jesus thought this idea of mine was "cute." I stood in perfect love and joy as I took in the wonder and beauty. And the dwelling, it's beyond description and it's mine.

They smiled. Loved shimmered in the air. Taking in more of the dwelling, I saw fields and structures and animals were everywhere. I love nature and animals. It's not a surprise my heavenly dwelling reflects my heart's desire.

Delight thyself also in the Lord:
and he shall give thee the desires of thine heart.
PSALM 37:4

I spoke to the Father as a child filled with glee without fear or shame, "Daddy, can I have horses?" Most of my life I've wanted a horse of my own. The Father knows this.

His response, "Of course, how about two hundred? Your friends can visit and ride with you."

More bawling. More laughter. Sheer joy and happiness. And Warrior friend, if you like to ride horses, you're invited to my place in the future! *grin*

And then too quickly my walk was over as I reached my car, and upon touching the door handle, the vision experience ended. I opened the door and scrambled around for a tissue.

I unpacked this experience with the Lord for weeks afterward. He brought clarity and purpose for this unique experience. "Lynn, I want you and those you serve to know that every sacrifice they make, all they endure, every tear, each and every prayer is building their dwelling in eternity. What my children say and do every single day creates. Every time you choose faith over fear and belief over doubt, hope over deception, you are placing another piece into the glorious dwelling place of your eternity."

It is real.

This encounter was life changing for me. A lifetime of

laying down my desires for my husband became beautiful flowers and horses. *grin* A life of serving in Bible study, raising kids to faith, a smile at the cashier at Walmart. A kind note sent in the mail and a blessing or prayer written in the comments of my blog, all of it is meaningful and holds purpose in the realm of the kingdom. Prayer by prayer, gold brick by gold brick.

GOODNESS OF GOD

The Lord is good to all: and his tender mercies
are over all his works.
PSALM 145:9

My dear friend, we place impossible demands upon ourselves, far exceeding God's expectations. He is so good, and I promise, he thinks we are amazing. His only request is for us to walk through our assignment on earth to the best of our ability. And our assignment is to learn to love. His goodness is everywhere. He is always speaking. He is always ready and waiting to give every good gift to us now and in eternity.

If our unbelieving spouse could catch us living in the lavish goodness of God continually, I'm convinced they would come screaming to the altar, begging for his/her baptism. We have God within us, Christ in us, the hope of glory. Release his goodness because it's the goodness of God that leads to repentance.

Or do you show contempt for the riches of his kindness,
forbearance and patience, not realizing that God's kindness is
intended to lead you to repentance?
ROMANS 2:4

Let go of your limited view of God and his goodness. We are being called to build higher, to serve, to love, and to experience God in spectacular encounters.

My Jericho Journal

DATE: _____

Ask the Lord to reveal what you are building.

After this I looked, and behold, a door standing open in heaven! And the first voice, which I had heard speaking to me like a trumpet, said, "Come up here….."
REVELATION 4:1

_____

_____

_____

_____

_____

_____

_____

_____

_____

_____

_____

_____

_____

_____

_____

_____

_____

_____

CHAPTER NINETEEN

Battle Cry

Joshua told the people, "Consecrate yourselves, for tomorrow the Lord will do amazing things among you."
JOSHUA 3:5

Consecrate:
To make holy or to dedicate to a higher purpose.

Freedom Fighter, this is a march into holiness. We are walking the narrow path of Matthew 7:13 toward a life of joy, love, and beauty. I know you desire to live in the fullness of the kingdom. I also know you are desperate for your spouse to taste and see that the Lord is good.

Welcome to the endgame.

The price of our arrival appears costly when viewed from the starting line. However, equipped with the tool belt of truth, coupled with our wilderness training, victory over Satan is at hand. Now is the time for the restoration of all things, the salvation of souls, starting with our spouse and children. There is little time to waste. Entrance into the theater of war is granted and now open before us. Follow the leading of Jesus as we cross into the Promised Land.

We are battle ready. Let's shout the war cry. WE ARE POWERFUL CHILDREN OF THE MOST HIGH GOD!

Our intimacy with the Lord determines our steps, and with each decree, we release the reconnaissance of angelic forces. Our honed character is well established in obedience, quick forgiveness, and repentance. The Word of God abides within and we wield the Sword with great authority. Our powerful voice sounds off and the devils shriek. Years of refining, pruning, surrender, followed by equipping with principals, vision, creative thought, and prophetic understanding we are ready to reveal the Lord of Hosts to a lost and broken world.

We are the light upon a hill (Matthew 5:14). The downtrodden and wounded are drawn to those of us who truly know God and walk in his purposes. It's nearly impossible for our unbelieving spouses to deny we are a new creation.

My battle year was an exercise in binding and loosing. I also spent time in repentance for generational sins and claiming scriptures with new revelation to the depths and the far-reaching possibilities they offer. This passage in Matthew is extraordinarily powerful. Memorize it and wield it often.

I will give you the keys of the kingdom of heaven; whatever you bind on earth will be bound in heaven, and whatever you loose on earth will be loosed in heaven.
MATTHEW 16:19

At some point within year six, I sensed a shift in Mike. I knew in my spirit he was a believer in Jesus yet hadn't professed his belief to me or anyone, for that matter. Also in year six, peace, mutual love, and respect became commonplace within our home. Our marriage relationship vastly improved. So much so, our adult children remarked at the change.

A shift in the spiritual realm also occurred once I released Mike from the label "unequally yoked." I stepped into a conviction we were equal as children of God. The only difference was one of us had trained longer than the other. Releasing my husband from this label somehow freed him from the bondage of defending his positions and worldview. And my sold-out, on-fire faith was on full display 24/7. He no longer was offended by faith, or my crazy faith-antics and conversations about God. Neither did my spontaneous prayers in Walmart or the healing and deliverance ministries where I served cause discord between us.

Something unexpected and wonderful happened in this season. A depth of love I didn't know was possible exploded in my heart. I clearly recall the exact moment the Lord allowed me to grasp the overwhelming affection alive within.

It was an ordinary day in the Donovan house. Mike was working in his office. I was clearing the table after breakfast. He'd left the kitchen table quickly to join a conference call. I overheard his muffled voice from down the hall as I stood over the table collecting plates.

In that precise moment, I noticed Mike had left his reading glasses, resting upside down, atop the table. In his haste, he'd forgotten them. As I stared at the glasses, an overwhelming familiarity of sharing a lifetime with this man swept over me. His black-rimmed readers represented a lifetime of love, memories, experiences shared with one man. A man who was with me in the good and the bad and in the difficult and sometimes impossible. A profound thankfulness arose within and consumed my heart. It's as though I felt inside every sacrifice Mike made for our marriage throughout the years. He loved me, really loved me. He is a loyal man and he honored and cherished me with all of himself and dedicated his life to protect and build our family and marriage.

Mike and I are far from perfect. Far from it. But staring at his glasses, tears welled. I gulped back emotion. I loved this man with more passion and fervor than I thought capable.

This once-broken, oppressed woman learned to love, forgive, fight in faith, and stand for what appeared unattainable. Waves of love crashed over my soul. My marriage vows were worth their price in gold. My love for my husband changed in a moment as I looked at those reading glasses, left forgotten.

~I learned to love.~

It wasn't long after this moment the final battle began. And after nearly three decades of prayer, God knew I was prepared. And my dream was within reach.

CROSSING THE JORDAN

The Lord told Joshua, "Today I will begin to make you a great leader in the eyes of all the Israelites. They will know that I am with you, just as I was with Moses."
JOSHUA 3:7

Happy New Year!

Each year in January, I lead a weeklong community fast through the online ministry where I serve. This fast ushers in the new year with powerful hope and faith. Believers from all over the world fast and pray together, seeking wisdom and revelation, as we petition for the salvation of our spouses. Many who fast receive a word of guidance or encouragement from the Lord for the year ahead. All except me. Not once in all the years of fasting. Nothing. Nada. Until the seventh year of my Jericho March.

My word: Divine Reversal.

During this particular fast, I was contemplating stepping away from my online ministry. After thirteen years of prolific writing, I felt as though I'd written about every unequally yoked marriage topic at least five different times. I remember praying in January, "God, I've said everything I have to say. I no longer feel called to lead this ministry. I know Mike believes in Jesus. And I feel as though I've arrived at the end of my service and have honored your name and my commitment."

I prayed intensely over this decision for most of December leading up to the fast. As I approached January, I felt peaceful about stepping away, or at least turning some of the writing over to other team members. I sensed God gave me peace over this decision. However, one thing felt unfinished.

Mike wasn't baptized.

For me, his baptism wasn't imperative. Because in my heart I'd resolved Mike was a believer in Jesus and a baptism wouldn't change anything. I was at peace regarding his salvation. Yet, I couldn't help praying about it.

> *Lord, I'm likely going to step away from this ministry you asked me to shoulder for more than thirteen years. Father, I'm absolutely fine with departing. I feel as though I've served to the best of my ability and I have nothing left unsaid.*

I could sense the Lord listening and his agreement. I continued:

> *But Lord, come on! It can't end like this. Father, through this ministry thousands of people have prayed for*

this one man's salvation. It can't conclude without a baptism. God, you are God. It just can't happen this way. The ending of thirteen years of ministry without a visible result will not glorify your name.

Father, you know deep in my heart I'm fine without a baptism because Mike believes, but God, are you?

I couldn't reconcile that God would prosper this ministry for many years without capping it off with a glorious move to validate all the ministry stands upon. However, it was totally up to God to bring this powerful conclusion to its rightful finish.

Up until this point, I'd only asked Mike about his faith sporadically, and hadn't inquired regarding his beliefs in months and months. And certainly, we hadn't discussed baptism in years. So, I'm telling you, on a cold January morning, the closing of the online ministry appeared unfinished and uninspired. Ugh!

I continued to pray along these lines throughout January. I settled it in my mind that my ministry service would draw down in the near future. But somehow it felt hollow.

Well, apparently the Lord agreed. With the arrival of February, I continued to pray, and in the first few days, God began to move. While standing in worship on a Monday evening at church, the first of special weeklong services, the resigning of ministry laid heavy upon my mind. In the midst of worship, I whispered, "God, what am I going to do about ending this ministry?"

Almost audibly, God intensely and sternly replied, "**This ends with a baptism.**"

I began to shake under his love and presence, knowing God replied and would defend his name. I immediately shared this revelation with my pastor and only about five other people. I told them what I heard and asked them to pray with me for this ending.

I will share with you this ending seemed utterly impossible from where I was standing in the moment. Remember I hadn't spoken to Mike about faith in months. But I began to ask God, "How?"

THE FALL OF JERICHO

Now when Joshua was near Jericho, he looked up and saw a man standing in front of him with a drawn sword in his hand. Joshua went up to him and asked, "Are you for us or for our enemies?"

"Neither," he replied, "but as commander of the army of the Lord I have now come." Then Joshua fell facedown to the ground in reverence, and asked him, "What message does my Lord have for his servant?"

The commander of the Lord's army replied, "Take off your sandals, for the place where you are standing is holy." And Joshua did so.
JOSHUA 5:13-15

"This ends with a baptism," continued to echo in my mind. I began to pray into this statement. I would decree these words during my prayer walks; God has sent forth His word and I stand in faith to see it fulfilled. I would ask the Lord, what was my place within this process? Gently, the Holy Spirit would lead me to pray God would provide an opportunity to discuss baptism with Mike.

And within a few days, the perfect opportunity arrived. Mike and I were seated at our favorite steakhouse. We placed our order, and while waiting, I broached the subject.

"So, I wanted to chat with you about something." He looked at me hesitantly. I continued on speaking matter-of-factly. "I know you believe in Jesus. I know you believe he walked on this planet and that he is the Son of God. I know you have believed this for a couple of years." I had his full attention. He silently agreed, so I pushed ahead.

"We've discussed for a while now that I'm considering departing the unequally yoked ministry in a couple of months." He nods. "I've been praying, and I feel as though I'm to ask you to consider being baptized. It seems like this is how this ministry comes to a close. What do you think?'

Yeah, I actually asked.

Mike replied, "Let me think about it."

Warriors, the ease of the conversation was of the Holy

Spirit, and to my astonishment, Mike didn't say no. He hadn't said yes either, but this was new territory. We hadn't been down this road before.

I was poised on holy ground. And the God of the universe and his angel armies were marching ahead of me. Was the Promised Land within view?

Two weeks passed. During this time the Lord cautioned me not to ask anything of Mike. God told me to pray. I prayed like crazy. One beautiful morning the Lord placed a name of a pastor on my heart. This was the man who, years prior, spent time with Mike in a class offered at our church for unbelievers. I spontaneously phoned him.

"Hi, Pastor." After pleasantries and a quick catch-up, I said, "Mike is a believer in Jesus. And he is considering becoming baptized. I've been praying and I have a giant favor to ask. Would you be willing to baptize him? All of those years ago when you poured into my husband's life, they were for this moment and Mike feels comfortable with you."

"Wow, that is fantastic, and I would be honored to baptize him."

I explained the process we were walking through and I would call to arrange a time for Mike's baptism, if and when he decided to move forward.

A week later, seated over dinner, "Mike, what are you thinking about the baptism? I'm reaching a place where I must make some decisions about the ministry."

"I'm still thinking about it."

I let Mike know I spoke with the pastor and then we spoke about making arrangements. We talked about what would happen at the baptism. I posed the question, "And you do understand he will ask you to confess your faith and state, Jesus is your savior?"

"Yes, I took the class. I know," he stated, matter-of-factly. Years earlier Mike enrolled in a skeptic's class at my church with the same pastor I phoned about his baptism. These seemingly small steps years prior truly were mustard seeds.

Warrior, when he replied with this answer, I KNEW he was honestly contemplating his decision. To my surprise, he mentioned the names of two other men who had spent time with him discussing faith and how they might want to be present if he was baptized. It was obvious. Mike was honestly considering this next step.

Wow. Truly we cannot underestimate the value of tiny seeds planted years ago and the power of God as he uses even small moments to impact people. The conversation concluded and I think I couldn't stop smiling inside. But I was playing it cool on the outside. By the way, dinner was fantastic.

Then things stalled.

My Jericho Journal

DATE:

How is God calling you into holiness? What is He speaking to you about the seeds he's planted? How is the Lord asking you to pray for your spouse? Your children?

CHAPTER TWENTY

Trembling Walls

*Joshua told the people, "**Consecrate yourselves, for tomorrow the Lord will do amazing things among you.**"*
JOSHUA 3:5

Two weeks dragged along in walled-up silence as Mike contemplated and said nothing. And in the silence, the enemy pounced.

It's always in the waiting, isn't it?

Predictably, the demonic attach to emotions of fear, uncertainty, and disappointment. Although I'd gained tremendous territory through my years of training, in this moment, following days that stretched on without a mention about baptism, the hope deferred began to intertwine with doubt. I questioned myself. Did I hear the Lord clearly? Did he really say to me, this ends with a baptism? Was that God's voice or was it me?

Ugh.

NO! Resist the devil and he shall flee. I refused to back down. I determined to believe. I chose to believe while facing the glaring reality, Mike might be permanently stalled.

I prayed and I prayed. "Lord, what is the delay? I know I heard your voice. But something is blocking him."

God replied, "Bring Mike before my court and ask for his forgiveness."

Whoa!

TEAR DOWN THE WALLS
OF UNFORGIVEN SIN

*For the unbelieving husband has been sanctified through his wife,
and the unbelieving wife has been sanctified through her believing
husband. Otherwise your children would be unclean,
but as it is, they are holy.*
1 CORINTHIANS 7:14

*If you forgive anyone's sins, their sins are forgiven; if you do not
forgive them, they are not forgiven.*
JOHN 20:23

God urged me to place a demand upon my faith and these
two scripture verses. Then intensely intercede for my husband.

Through years of studying the scriptures, I became familiar with the Lord's voice. He brought passages before me through
my daily Bible reading, asking me questions. For example, Jesus
and I spent significant time in prayerful conversation over the
implications of 1 Corinthians 7:14.

"Lynn, how far-reaching is the possibility of this verse?
I want you to contemplate the vastness, the sheer possibility of
what this passage offers you, your husband, and children."

I began to pray daily, standing in faith upon the truth
of this passage. My faith in this passage grew. I fully believed
my spouse and children are sanctified, set apart as holy unto the
Lord. As my faith grew, so did the possibilities. So, I prayed as
though each family member was indeed set apart and included
in the plans of God. I would bless them with provision, opportunity, increase, and pray to release them from oppression, fear,
or hopelessness.

On days when my children telephoned looking for encouragement to face whatever difficulty was before them, I would
hang up the phone and then take them to the king. I would stand
upon this passage believing and declaring their release and inclusion into the heavenly decrees over their lives. I believed
this verse as a literal depiction of my faith and family, and then
stretched its possibility to the fullest in my prayers. After all,
what was there to lose? A few breaths and some uttered words.

This is the faith-life that moves mountains. My conviction was absolute which demanded the heavenly realms respond to my utterances of prayers of intercession merely because I asked. I was standing on the truth the Bible assures is available to those who are unequally yoked.

I began to press into multiple passages in a similar manner in full faith. I would pray them, quote them, and stand upon them with my declarations, executing them into place through prayer and faith. I would join my desires to the desires of my Father, willing his purpose forward on earth as it is in heaven.

And on the day the Lord told me to take my husband into court, I already knew the scripture passages I would stand upon. 1 Corinthians 7:14 and John 20:23.

So, I did exactly that!

Taking My Spouse into the Courtroom of God

If you forgive anyone's sins, their sins are forgiven; if you do not forgive them, they are not forgiven.
JOHN 20:23

When Jesus brought this scripture to me, I went into some study. The Greek translation of forgive sins is set free. Hallelujah. I wouldn't have thought this possible a few months prior. However, during my prayer time, Jesus asked me a question when I read John 20:23. "Lynn, did I not tell the disciples they could pray and ask me to set people free? Is it not clearly in the Word? Are you my disciple?"

"Yes."

On this particular morning, the Lord spoke, "I want you to stand in proxy for your husband, claiming 1 Corinthians 7:14 and John 20:23 as your authority to intercede and ask for forgiveness on behalf of Mike."

I opened my Bible and read the passages again. Yep, indeed Jesus is instructing the disciples to intercede to set people free. I also read the petitions made by Daniel on behalf of the people of God who were held in Babylonian captivity.

In the first year of Darius son of Xerxes (a Mede by descent), who was made ruler over the Babylonian kingdom—in the first year of his reign, I, Daniel, understood from the Scriptures, according to the word of the Lord given to Jeremiah the prophet, that the desolation of Jerusalem would last seventy years. So I turned to the Lord God and pleaded with him in prayer and petition, in fasting, and in sackcloth and ashes.

I prayed to the Lord my God and confessed:

"Lord, the great and awesome God, who keeps his covenant of love with those who love him and keep his commandments, we have sinned and done wrong. We have been wicked and have rebelled; we have turned away from your commands and laws. We have not listened to your servants the prophets, who spoke in your name to our kings, our princes and our ancestors, and to all the people of the land.

"Lord, you are righteous, but this day we are covered with shame—the people of Judah and the inhabitants of Jerusalem and all Israel, both near and far, in all the countries where you have scattered us because of our unfaithfulness to you. We and our kings, our princes and our ancestors are covered with shame, Lord, because we have sinned against you.
The Lord our God is merciful and forgiving,
even though we have rebelled against him."
DANIEL 9:1-9

If Daniel petitioned God seeking his mercy and Jesus instructed the disciples to intercede to set people free, then it was worth the effort to try.

I arrived at the time and place where everything I learned, the authority I walked in, and the power of the Holy Spirit which dwelled within, culminated in the war of wars. The devil vs. God, and the prize, my husband's future baptism.

I stood upon these scriptures. I placed them before the Lord and then entered his court and asked the accuser to appear and present his accusations against my husband.

Immediately I began to hear the accusations. As the accusations arrived in my mind, I began to pray.

"In the name of Jesus, I stand on behalf of my husband

upon 1 Corinthians 7:14. I sanctify my husband and set him apart for the Lord. I take authority over him through my faith as the believing wife. I now stand upon John 20:23 and I intercede on his behalf."

Accusations began to roll. First, I heard Dungeons and Dragons. I immediately began to intercede, asking for God to forgive his involvement in role-playing games, where he took on demonic personalities. I interceded for his belief in science as a god. I prayed and asked God to forgive Mike for listening to other voices as his truth instead of God. I asked the Lord to forgive him for rejecting Christ. Offenses arose from his distant past as well as those in his present. Any sin brought to my mind, I stood as a family representative, his wife and life partner and believer, and I interceded, asking the Lord to forgive him and set him free, calling on the John 20:23 passage as my authority as well as 1 Corinthians 7:14.

I prayed aloud, interceding for each sin to be removed from his record, washed away by the redeeming blood of Christ. I asked for his restoration into his destiny and position as a son of God. I prayed and I prayed. I forgave him from my heart, and I petitioned the Lord to bring Mike to repentance as well.

Finally, the accusations ceased. It was finished. I felt peace. I knew that my prayers were being used by God to release Mike from the accusations of the enemy and to prepare his heart for freedom through faith in Jesus Christ.

I determined to stand upon the scriptures and my faith in action for the benefit of my husband.

All I could do now was believe and then wait and see what God did next.

My friend, how far-reaching is scripture? Does anyone truly know the depth, the reach or full purposes of God? Who is to say we can or cannot bring others before God through our love relationship and our intimacy with the Father and ask for mercy and forgiveness? Why would Jesus command such a thing if it wasn't truly possible? From my perspective, I will not limit God nor place him in a box, ever! I've lived long enough and bear witness to the fact, God will defy the pundits.

God provided specific instructions to me on how and

what to pray as I interceded for my husband. I believed and obeyed.

My dear friend, I'm sharing my experience with you about the courts of heaven and standing on scripture, but it's faith and your free-will which empowers your prayers before the Lord. Your heart condition must align with truth and exercise your faith, choosing to believe. I'm sharing what's been made available through the Word. Believe and receive.

My Jericho Journal

DATE: _____

     John 20:23 is a powerful aspect of faith the body of Christ has, for the most part, overlooked. Today, I gift you this wonderful passage. Bring this passage before the Lord into his courtroom and seek justice and forgive those for whom you are praying for their salvation.

     Pray for your spouse and others aloud and by name.

     I bless you to experience the wonder and fullness of the Word of God, alive and in action in your life today. In Jesus's name, AMEN

_____

_____

_____

_____

_____

_____

_____

_____

_____

_____

_____

_____

_____

_____

Chapter Twenty-One
Crumbling Walls

On the seventh day, they got up at daybreak and marched around the city seven times in the same manner, except that on that day they circled the city seven times. The seventh time around, when the priests sounded the trumpet blast, Joshua commanded the army,

"Shout! For the Lord has given you the city!"
JOSHUA 6:15-16

February passed while I waited and prayed, consistently engaging my prayer language. Still my husband remained silent about any decision.

In early March the Lord spoke to me. He said, "Lynn, your entire ministry has been centered around your marriage. I want to give you a special blessing, as a sweet kiss from me, your Father. Ask the pastor if you can arrange Mike's baptism on your wedding anniversary, March 14th.

Whoa. I nearly bawled my eyes out. What a beautiful and kind gift this would be from my Father. So, I phoned the church and asked the pastor for another large, really large, ask. March 14th at 2 p.m.

It was all arranged.

Yet, Mike hadn't agreed. Gulp. This is real faith. In this season I battled the enemy with all I had learned from my tool belt and marching years. I stood in faith. I took authority over doubt and deceptions. I exercised my power in the Holy Spirit to move all of earth if necessary, to open the door to this endgame victory.

I felt weary from the praying. I was worn out swinging my sword of faith. I was applying absolutely every tool I possessed into the coming collision of good versus evil over my husband.

I was standing in the middle of the battleground with my armor clad around me and swiveling my sword. I'd lived twenty-seven years in faith in preparation for this final showdown. And my warrior friend, I wasn't going to settle for a defeat.

Finally, I mentioned the scheduled baptism to Mike while seated at our favorite restaurant. This was when the most beautiful conversation ensued.

"I'm a bit concerned if I do this (baptism) your expectations are that I would become like you." From his perspective, I'm a freak of nature. I have walked with God for three decades. I'm scary and I love that I am. Yet, Mike isn't designed to be like me.

I said to him, "I have zero expectations of you. You do you and your faith. I'll do me. You don't need to attend church to make me happy. I won't place any demand upon you in the future with regard to faith. I'm so very content with where we are and where I am."

He smiled. And then he agreed!

Hallelujah. Did that just happen?

I called the church. It was all arranged.

Then, twenty-four hours prior, all hell broke loose.

ONLY GOD

Let us hold unswervingly to the hope we profess,
for he who promised is faithful.
HEBREWS 10:23

Exactly at two o' clock in the afternoon, on the day prior to the scheduled baptism, Mike received the news that drastic changes were underway with his employer. In an abrupt and unscheduled decision, the company informed him, he was being released from his current work assignment. All of a sudden it looked as though a layoff was imminent.

I stood in the door of his home office, shocked as he

shared the news. To the breadwinner of the family, this news is, of course, devastating. Emotions run high—fear, confusion, anger, just to name a few. In a split second, a number of thoughts rushed into my mind. *This is of the enemy. This is a direct attack to frighten Mike. The enemy is creating confusion and fear in an effort to lock him in his office, afraid to leave as he tries to reverse this decision. He won't go to the church tomorrow.*

I hate the enemy.

I was leaving for a scheduled prayer appointment at my church. I looked directly at him and the spirit of the Lord arose within me and I stated with complete faith, "Mike, you know this is an attack of the enemy. I'm declaring God will show you a divine reversal." (Remember, divine reversal was the word the Lord gave me in January.) "The enemy is NOT going to get away with this. In Jesus's name."

I kissed him and said I would return right after the prayer session. I jumped into the car and let loose my mouth in prayer and I destroyed every demonic assault we faced. I chained up the demons with my words, lit them on fire, then sent them to the pit. I called all of heaven to issue a divine reversal of this attack against my husband. I spoke to my Father and reminded him of the many promises that were mine. I called to arms a large number of the angelic and sent them to destroy every work of the devil. I prayed. I believed. I issued decrees and I took authority over every assignment coming against my man. In Jesus's name, AMEN

Returning home from a fantastic prayer session, I walked into Mike's office. "Let's go get some ice cream." I felt like it would help to get his mind off the fear and uncertainty.

"No, we don't need to do that."

"Yes, I want to go. Let's forget about all this for now."

"I just received a call from another manager and they are placing me on a new project."

I gawked.

Divine Reversal!

God is good. God is powerful. God is our shield and comfort. God cares about every detail in our lives. AMEN.

We need to pray like we believe it!

CAPTIVES SET FREE
MARCH 14

Jesus said: "The Spirit of the Lord is on me, because he has anointed me to proclaim good news to the poor. He has sent me to proclaim freedom for the prisoners and recovery of sight for the blind, to set the oppressed free, to proclaim the year of the Lord's favor."

Then he rolled up the scroll, gave it back to the attendant and sat down. The eyes of everyone in the synagogue were fastened on him. He began by saying to them,

"Today this scripture is fulfilled in your hearing."
LUKE 4:18

We both jumped into the car. I looked at him, "Are you nervous?"

"No, you?"

"Yes. I'm a wreck."

"Did you think I would change my mind?"

"Yes."

He smiled at me. I smiled back. We chuckled, then we drove off toward the church for a divine appointment, twenty-seven years in the making. I'd prayed fervently for nearly most of the night and day leading up to this. But now here we were driving toward destiny.

It felt surreal. Was this really happening and on our anniversary?

We arrived and the baptismal was readied, full of warm water. The pastor, along with one of my oldest and dearest friends with whom I serve in women's ministry, sat down with us. Mike explained how he arrived at this decision and then the moment arrived.

"Do you believe Jesus is the Son of God and do you accept him as your Lord and Savior?" the pastor asked Mike.

"Yes."

I cried. My ministry friend rejoiced and snapped a few pictures. The pastor beamed. Jesus smiled. God loved and the Holy Spirit gained a new friend.

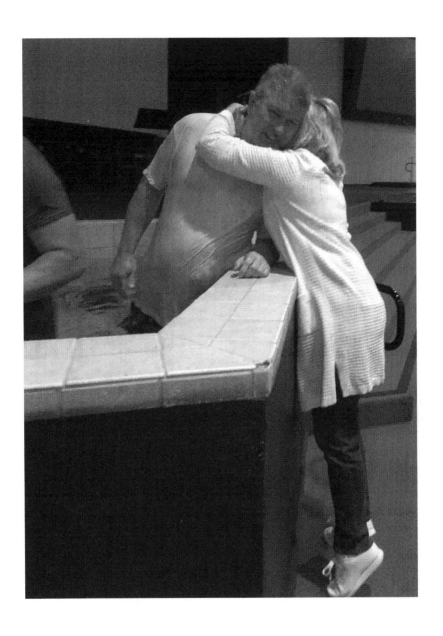

CHAPTER TWENTY-TWO

The Trumpet Sounds

*When the trumpets sounded, the army shouted, and at the sound of the trumpet, when the men gave a loud shout, **the wall collapsed**; so everyone charged straight in, and they took the city. They devoted the city to the Lord.*
JOSHUA 6:20-21a

Of course, our marriage and faith journey continue. Mike and I are well loved by the Lord.

As of the writing of this book, my seven-year march around Jericho is drawing to completion. This book is the final step in this glorious march with the Lord and my husband. The ending far exceeded anything I could hope or dream. And now I step into a new season. I can't wait. I'm expectant of greater things because God is just that good.

It's time, dearest friend. Latch your tool belt about your waist then take your first step across the line of no return. The journey is arduous and lengthy. But the supernatural gifts of God are a worthy pursuit. He must always be our lifelong focus. And when he is, everything else falls into place.

I'm your biggest cheerleader as you start your march. I am praying for you from the depths of my soul for your victories. But, more than mere victories in our earthly life, I'm praying for the transformation of your heart.

I kneel before the Father, from whom every family in heaven and on earth derives its name. I pray that out of his glorious riches he may strengthen you with power through his Spirit in your inner being, so that Christ may dwell in your hearts through faith. And I pray that you, being rooted and established in love, may have power, together with all the Lord's holy people, to grasp how wide and long and high and deep is the love of Christ, and to know this love that surpasses knowledge—that you may be filled to the measure of all the fullness of God.

Now to him who is able to do immeasurably more than all we ask or imagine, according to his power that is at work within us, to him be glory in the church and in Christ Jesus throughout all generations, for ever and ever! Amen.

****

Nothing in this book is possible outside of the love and favor of God. He alone is the answer to every question humanity faces, throughout all the ages. Jesus is the savior and redeemer of humanity and all of creation. He is our healer, our deliverance, freedom, and truth. The Holy Spirit is our friend and comforter, our protector.

I truly believe my Jericho March experience is a guide for others who are living in a spiritually mismatched marriage. It's a model of kingdom living. This is a guide into truth, and it is for all people. Although I can't guarantee your story will turn out like mine, I will promise you this: Your earnest pursuit through the lessons contained in this book will lead you into realms of glory that leave you breathless, fill your heart, heal every wound, and seat you with Christ in heavenly realms. Your life will never be the same and it's all glory!

We are kingdom people living in a pinnacle of time and space. Casual Christianity is no longer an option. Once-a-week church will not suffice. Those of us who hunger and thirst for the king must press in with eager anticipation and relentless pounding on the door of heaven, asking for more.

Greater revelations of love, peace, and joy are for those who seek. Miracles, signs, and wonders will accompany all those who linger with the king in his chamber and meet with him, kneeling before the Throne of Grace.

My warrior friend, the last seven years of my faith-life never was about my husband. However, because my faith came alive in our home, God changed him. My husband could no longer deny the presence of the Trinity dwelling within. How can a mere mortal man resist the power and love of the God of the universe when displayed through his wife, or a husband?

You are filled with unlimited power and authority. You are graced with lavish provision, weaponry, vast instruction and accompanied by all of heaven. You merely need to declare: I'm in!

March on, Warrior! WE WIN!

The end...or is it just the beginning?

Resources

Marching Around Jericho is your blueprint to pray your unsaved spouse into the Kingdom of God. It contains powerful lessons that lead to transformation in your faith, your life, and marriage.

For those who hunger and thirst for more of the Kingdom, the author has created teaching modules which expand on the concepts and lessons in the book.

Commit yourself as a Warrior for Kingdom and accelerate your faith.

The modules include:

MODULE ONE:
INTIMACY & IDENTITY

Intimacy with the Father
(The Goodness of God)

Intimacy with Jesus

Hearing the Voice of God
(This module is free for viewing and PDF download.)

Kingdom Identity

Original Design

Module Two: Partnering with the Holy Spirit

The Power of Forgiveness

Spiritual Authority in Christ Jesus

Spiritual Power and Partnering with the Holy Spirit

The Power of Our Voice

Speaking in Tongues

Module Three: Understanding the Demonic

Who Is Our Enemy?

Legal Rights

Generational Curses/Word Curses/Land Curses

The Occult

Witchcraft

Module Four: Kingdom Lifestyle

Lifestyle of Thankfulness and Hope

Power of Blessing & Peace

Power of Love & Worship

Facing Setbacks

Courts of Heaven

Module Five:
Kingdom Life

Lifestyle of Holiness

Lifestyle & Benefits of Quick Obedience

Healing & Deliverance for Self and Others

Community Living

Friendship

Friendships

The module's curriculum includes a worksheet, activation, homework, questions, and is accompanied by video teaching by the author. This is transformative teaching that will increase your faith and grow your confidence. Expect greater encounters with Jesus Christ and intimacy with the Father which will lead to individual breakthroughs and truth. Download the first module for free

And if you desire to launch your journey onto the super-fast track, consider signing up for an individual spiritual development/coaching session. You can find these resources and more at Marchingaroundjericho.com

The future is yours, Warrior! You are a child of the King!

Read Lynn's Other Books

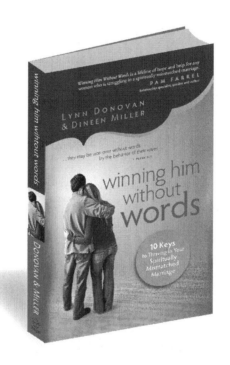

WINNING HIM WITHOUT WORDS
By Lynn Donovan & Dineen Miller

FROM THREE KEYS PUBLISHING:

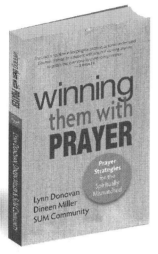

WINNING THEM WITH PRAYER
By Lynn Donovan & Dineen Miller

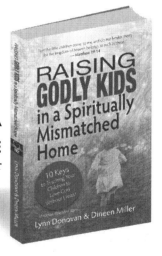

RAISING GODLY KIDS IN A SPIRITUALLY MISMATCHED HOME
By Lynn Donovan & Dineen Miller

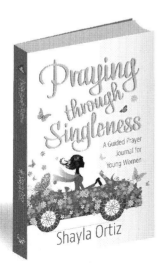

PRAYING THROUGH SINGLENESS
By Shayla Ortiz

Made in the USA
Columbia, SC
15 October 2021

47272263R00124